JAMES BOND
MOVIE POSTERS

THE OFFICIAL 007 COLLECTION

JAMES BOND

MOVIE POSTERS

Tony Nourmand

BOXTREE

First published 2001 by Boxtree, an imprint of Pan Macmillan Ltd
Pan Macmillan, 20 New Wharf Road, London N1 9RR
Basingstoke and Oxford
Associated companies throughout the world
www.panmacmillan.com

ISBN 0 7522 2017 9

Designed by Bradbury and Williams

9 8 7 6 5 4 3 2 1

A CIP catalogue record for this book is available from the British Library

Printed by the Bath Press, Bath.

Author's Acknowledgements

Editorial Assistant Kim Goddard

Thanks to Professor Christopher Frayling
Joseph Caroff
Ellen De Wachter
Bruce Marchant
Graham Marsh
Hy Smith

From Russia With Love US set of 4, each 60 x 20 inches, from the collection of Roberto Hoornweg
Casino Royale US Set of 6, each 60 x 20 inches, from the collection of John Myhre

Contents

Foreword

An animated white circle moves across a blank screen – like the focusing of a camera, or maybe like a range finder – until it turns into what could be the iris of a camera lens but is in fact the rifled circle of a gun barrel; two different kinds of shooting. A well-dressed man in a hat walks into the circle, turns and fires a shot at it – or rather at us, the audience. The rifle barrel is saturated by a curtain of blood red, before turning back into a white circle again. The movie begins. After an elaborate and usually self-contained prologue, the credit titles are woven around the seductive silhouettes of nude females gyrating and doing suggestive things with hi-tech weapons. The opening gun barrel logo, and the 'kiss kiss bang bang' main titles, have over the last forty years or so become the corporate images – or visual signatures – for the most successful franchise in the history of the movies. They are up there with Mickey Mouse's rounded ears and the outline of Alfred Hitchcock's portly shape.

Both of these images had low-key origins. In the case of the gun barrel, producer Cubby Broccoli recalled that he gave graphic designer Maurice Binder all of fifteen minutes to come up with a concept that would embody the essence of James Bond in a few brief seconds of screen time, before summoning him to an important *Dr. No* production meeting: '[Binder] produced a couple of scraps of paper with some squiggles on them, and we had our Bond titles.' In the case of the sinuous credits, designer Robert Brownjohn used to dine out on the story of how the titles of *From Russia With Love* came about. The credits of *Dr. No* had featured bouncing, coloured dots and rotascoped Jamaican dancers, but for the second James Bond film something rather more confident and stylish was required. Brownjohn presented his concept to producers Broccoli and Harry Saltzman by taking off his shirt in a darkened room and dancing in a beam of light while a slide of white lettering was projected onto his naked back: 'for the real thing,' he said, 'it'll be just like this only we'll use a pretty girl.' This was to turn into the classic credits sequence in which the main titles were indeed projected onto the body of a pretty girl, that of a Turkish belly-dancer. Apparently, she had to eat a lot of bananas, to give her instant active energy, for her moment of screen fame.

Madison Avenue graphic style was meeting a very British kind of romantic anti-hero. But Brownjohn was trained as a modernist at the Chicago Institute – and the idea of projected lettering was a distant echo of the 'light play' films of Hungarian avant-garde designer Lazlo Moholy-Nagy, so the visuals were in fact part-European. These trademark images on the screen were matched by equally distinctive poster artwork in the cinema foyer and on hoardings outside, which sometimes conjugated with them in a direct way. It is surprising, therefore, that although there have been countless books about the James Bond films – reference books, monographs on the heroes and on the girls, accounts of 'the making of', studies of the adaptation from books to films, a major catalogue on production designer Ken Adam, even a book about Bond's style in menswear called *The Suited Hero* – there has never before been a substantial English-language book on the James Bond posters. After all, it was these front-of-house visuals – in all their international variations – that helped entice the paying customers to see the films in the first place. These days, a franchise that survives for two or three big-budget sequels is considered a marketing miracle. If the James Bond franchise went in for numbers – *Rocky* – or *Godfather*– or *Alien*-style – *The World Is Not Enough* would have been an astonishing *Bond 19* (or maybe *Bond 21* depending on how you count).

My introduction to the visual packaging of James Bond wasn't via the movies but from the jackets of the hardback books from the mid-1950s to the mid-1960s. My father bought *Casino Royale* at London Airport in 1953 – he liked casinos a lot – and I read it much too early, when I was an impressionable eleven-year-old. The dust jacket was boring: a traditional playing card with red hearts on a light purple background, plus the words 'a whisper of love... a whisper of hate' entwined around a yellow wreath, and a line drawing of Ian Fleming on the back. But the heady mixture of snobbery, sex and violence within (something very nasty with a fly-swatter) was a very different experience. I was hooked. Much more stylish dust jackets began with *From Russia With Love* in 1957: a watercolour handgun and a rose, lying on a grainy wooden background and drawn with meticulous care by the British illustrator Richard Chopping. This was, it later transpired, a world away from the in-your-face graphics of the movie posters, but it seemed just right for the books. *Goldfinger* (1959) followed with trompe l'oeil skull and gold coins in its eyes, a rose in its teeth, again on the distinctive grainy wooden base; *Thunderball* (1961) had a carnation, a knife and a handwritten note burned along its edges; *On Her Majesty's Secret Service* (1963) had a herald's hand designing Bond's coat of arms with its motto 'The World Is Not Enough' plus the title stamped on the wood as if it was an official parcel delivery; *You Only Live Twice* (1964), my favourite among the book jackets, had a Japanese-style toad killing a dragonfly, and a pink chrysanthemum, all laid out on a bamboo surface. I worked with Dickie Chopping at the Royal College of Art through the 1970s and early 1980s, and enjoyed reminiscing about these memorable and subtle designs; he later gave me one of his watercolours as a wedding present.

The year 1964 was the annus mirabilis of the James Bond films. *Dr. No* and *From Russia With Love* had already been released, and *Goldfinger* opened at the Odeon Leicester Square. I saw it the day after the première and joined in the applause as Oddjob met a sticky end – thanks to his metallized bowler hat – in Ken Adam's outrageously over-the-top Fort Knox, while the seconds ticked away. I had never heard an audience applauding a movie before. The poster (both versions) was designed by Robert Brownjohn as a frozen version of his credit titles: a shapely torso painted gold (a model in a bra standing in for Shirley Eaton) with a grainy photographic image of Sean Connery and Honor Blackman superimposed on it, and elegant gold, pink and white lettering down the right-hand side. The alternative version had an upright golden hand with superimposed James Bond and Pussy Galore. It was a classy, restrained piece of artwork that matched Brownjohn's animated titles for the movie itself: stills of golden hands and bodies and faces, with scenes from *Goldfinger* (and the helicopter featured in *From Russia With Love*) projected onto them, the outline shapes carefully matching the action they reflected. Maurice Binder liked to work with female models doing daring manoeuvres, and to involve a lot of action. Brownjohn preferred to film luxurious stills. The two earlier Bond posters had been more straightforward. The anonymous *Dr. No* had Sean Connery in a dinner jacket on the left-hand side with his pistol plus silencer pointing downwards in one hand and a cigarette in the other, flanked by four girls in various states of undress – like a coloured-in newspaper strip of the day accompanied by the redundant headline 'The first James Bond film!'. The similar American version added the 007 logo with gun extending from the '7' (created by Joseph Caroff), and the tagline 'Meet the most extraordinary gentleman spy in all fiction....' The 'gentleman spy' image – dinner jacket, licence to kill, expense account, smoothie pose, merciless air, ladykiller look, handgun – has survived more or less intact through various incarnations for the last forty years. In the 1940s or 1950s, it would have been the image of a villain – the suave sophisticate who was suspicious because he spoke correct English – but in *Dr. No*, he was played by a working-class Scotsman. The graphically more interesting *From Russia With Love* poster, by the Rome-based Renato Fratini, had the dinner-jacketed and self-assured

British 30 x 40 in (76 x 102 cm)
(Advance)
Artist/Illustrator Robert McGinnis and Frank McCarthy

Sean Connery in the centre, his handgun raised this time, surrounded by distilled highlights of the movie's action: gypsy girls fighting, a Turkish belly-dancer, Daniela Bianchi in a nightdress, and a helicopter over San Sofia in Istanbul, plus a locomotive steaming towards a car on the line. The film itself included a neat poster in-joke: the nasty Russian assassin emerged from the huge open mouth of Anita Ekberg – part of a wall advertisement for Saltzman and Broccoli's earlier *Call Me Bwana* (1963) – only to be shot down by Pedro Armendariz as the local spymaster working for 'our' side.

If the credit titles came into their own with *From Russia With Love* (as was the case with the book jackets), the posters came of age with *Goldfinger*. After that, they were to become increasingly elaborate and frenetic – 'everything Bond touches', as the American tagline for the movie put it, 'turns to excitement'. The celebrated series designed by graphics specialists Robert McGinnis and Frank McCarthy with United Artists advertising director Donald E. Smolen, and starting with *Thunderball* (1965), surrounded the spy in the dinner jacket with hyper-realistic scenes of explosions, gadgets doing their thing, and hand-to-hand combat – 'Look up! Look down!' James Bond does it everywhere!' Half-naked starlets at his feet made the tagline even more suggestive – boys' stuff for the *Playboy* generation, set five minutes into the future. As the production values soared, so the posters kept upping the ante. They also picked up on the increasingly sly tongue-in-cheek central performance. For *Thunderball*, the spy wore red rubber diving gear – but he was probably wearing his uncreased dinner jacket underneath it. The dangerous fashion models and even more dangerous consumer goodies depicted in these posters seemed to turn the myth of the Swinging Sixties on its head, while at the same time promoting it – with the emphasis on the audience being shaken rather than stirred. *You Only Live Twice* (1967) featured Ken Adams's missile base inside a Japanese volcano, plus Bond clutching a space helmet. *On Her Majesty's Secret Service* (1969) had George Lazenby being pursued across the snow by helicopters and exploding baddies on skis. Robert McGinnis's solo posters for *Diamonds Are Forever* (1971), *Live And Let Die* (1973) and *The Man With The Golden Gun* (1974) straddled the Sean Connery/Roger Moore eras with images of satellites and space stations, an exploding ship, a single gold bullet being loaded into a solid gold pistol and in the case of *Live And Let Die* a blazing bazooka that looked as though it was being fired from between James Bond's legs. This cycle came to an end with *The Man With The Golden Gun*, but the successful visual formula was developed, usually by designer Dan Gouzee, up to *A View To A Kill* (1985) and Roger Moore's retirement. For the *Moonraker* (1979) poster, Bond wore an astronaut's outfit and his weapon of choice was a spacegun, but his dinner jacket was visible just beneath the collar. In Japan, the formula was transformed into bold red characters for the names, a strong emphasis on the 007 logo and a collage of action photos: this 'look' was remarkably consistent.

The arrival of Timothy Dalton in *The Living Daylights* (1987) brought with it the original gun-barrel logo – featured on posters for the first time – as if the series was hoping to touch base. More recently, with Pierce Brosnan and the relaunch of the franchise through *GoldenEye* (1995), the marketing has taken on a more glossy, computerized look with the digits 007 given extra prominence next to a big photographic portrait of the window display hero.

For the first few years of the franchise's life, there were many substitute spies with substitute graphics: the mainstream ones were called Flint, or Solo, or Helm, or Love, or Blaise, or even Drummond. In Italy, countless Cinecittà agents with numerals on their labels tried to find a hip Mediterranean equivalent to the Bondage of the originals. I can remember one, a film called *Operation Kid Brother*, with Sean Connery's brother Neil in the lead role and a poster that tried hard to resemble that of *Thunderball*. But the last man standing was always James Bond, who managed to survive and develop through the dismantling of the Berlin Wall, the rejection by environmentalists of unbridled technology, the rise of the women's movement and the appointment of a female to manage MI6, the decline of the Soviet empire, the ascendancy of America as sole superpower, and the strictures of political correctness: a unique achievement within popular culture.

This book, assembled by Tony Nourmand with his characteristic skill, knowledge and insight, is a thorough visual record in poster form of forty years of collectible James Bond, forty years of a particular graphic language. As the tagline for *GoldenEye* put it: 'No substitutes…'

Professor Christopher Frayling
Rector of the Royal College of Art
July 2001

Introduction

French 31 x 24 in (79 x 61 cm)
(Red Strip)
Artist/Illustrator Jean Mascii

From the earliest days of cinema, over a century ago, film posters have been designed simply to attract audiences to movie theatres. Along with the medium of the radio, the advent of television in the fifties provided another arena in which studios could advertise films; today the internet also plays a major role in such merchandising. However, the film poster's importance as a method of advertising declined with the growth of television, which also led to a fall in the number of cinema-goers. As a result, there has been a slow decline in the quality of film poster design over the last fifty years. Of course there are always exceptions to the rule.

Author Ian Fleming introduced James Bond in the first of his twelve best-selling Bond novels, *Casino Royale*, based on his own experiences as an intelligence agent. Initially the James Bond character was also taken into a new dimension of fantasy via his serialization in a comic strip. Then, in 1962, the first Bond film *Dr. No* launched the most successful series of films ever produced.

Spanning forty years and five actors (six if you include David Niven in *Casino Royale*), Bond has retained his sex appeal and his popularity, due in large part to the idiosyncratic combination of a daring nature and the charming, even old-fashioned manners, stereotypical of an English gentleman. He has become every man's hero and every woman's fantasy. Bond's appeal has remained universal from the very first cinematic outing; and even today, almost anyone from any generation can name their favourite Bond.

The Bond films provide a breath of fresh air at a time when political correctness has become all-encompassing, an opportunity to fantasize – which, after all, is what the cinema is all about. Their tongue-in-cheek humour has allowed Bond, especially in Roger Moore's interpretation of the character, to push the boundaries of PC without causing offence. And whatever Bond's doing, it must be working, for he has become one of the greatest cultural icons of recent times.

Dr. No was the blueprint for the design and style of the subsequent films. Producers Albert R. Broccoli and Harry Saltzman hired a highly talented creative team that, by and large, went on to contribute to the rest of the series. Ken Adam designed the elaborate and innovative sets. Maurice Binder was responsible for the distinctive Bond titles; his opening gun barrel sequence was adapted to feature in all subsequent films in the series. Director Terence Young contributed to Bond's stylish dress sense, his manners and etiquette. The diverse creative input for the Bond films has resulted in a successful, high-quality run of no fewer than 21 films. And Bond shows no sign of wanting to retire just yet...

Traditionally, film posters were designed in-house, at the studios, and would accompany films from cinema to cinema; thereafter, the surviving posters were returned to the studios. Whenever studios needed to clear space, film posters would be systematically destroyed, as they had served their purpose. Consequently, just a fraction of the amount produced has survived.

Over the last decade, a market has emerged for original vintage film posters. Indeed, major auction houses now dedicate entire sales to this area. Film poster enthusiasts collect posters according to various themes – perhaps the film itself, its director, or the poster's illustrator, as well as by genres such as horror, sci-fi and film noir. Bond has created its own genre in movie posters, in the same way that it has carved out its own niche in cinema history. This genre has become one of the most popular, and is collected by people of all ages and from all walks of life. Inevitably, as these posters are purchased, the number of posters available on the open market decreases, to the extent that today the more highly sought after Bond posters have begun to fetch the same amounts as lithographs by celebrated artists such as Toulouse Lautrec or Alphonse Maria Mucha.

Many of the classic images and symbols of Bond that have now become part of our popular culture were introduced through film posters. Viewers first encountered the 007 logo by Joseph Caroff on the poster for *Dr. No*. The famous image of Bond with a gun across his chest, created by Eric Pulford, appeared initially on the poster for *From Russia With Love* in 1963, while Robert Brownjohn's golden girl image was first seen on the poster for *Goldfinger*. These images, along with some very catchy tag lines, have become some of the most memorable visual teasers in cinematic history.

Posters from a particular country can usually be distinguished by certain national characteristics but Bond posters always pushed the boundaries. Italian film posters were usually far sexier than most others, yet Bond posters introduced this risqué element worldwide, even in more conservative countries such as Britain and America. In Japan, a photomontage technique was used in the majority of their Bond campaigns, a peculiarity of that country. All of these designs were executed after telephone surveys had been carried out in different countries, to discover what audiences were attracted to. Hy Smith, the international Head of Publicity for United Artists, remembers that 'Moore's Bond actually did better in Japan than Connery's because they loved the lighter hair.'

Every film poster says something about the culture in which it was designed, and Bond posters are no exception. The very titles of the films have been through some weird and wonderful changes: for example, in France *From Russia With Love* was called *Hearty Kisses From Russia*, while in Japan *You Only Live Twice* became *007 Dies Twice (!)* and *Live And Let Die* was known as *The Dead Slave*. Bond's image is adapted to suit various national preconceptions in different campaigns worldwide. In the United States he is generally given a more casual appearance, while in Britain he is usually seen wearing a tuxedo. In stark contrast, Bond has also been seen in some South American campaigns with a more rugged five-o-clock shadow.

Naturally, Bond posters always featured the elements that made the films successful – often including scantily clad women or potentially violent images. These images would sometimes encounter opposition in more conservative or religious countries, such as Ireland, Spain and the USA. As a result, many Bond poster designs had to be censored or withdrawn. And that wasn't enough for some people: from time to time, pedestrians or cinema owners would cover up what they believed to be offensive images.

Still, there's no doubting the part the posters played in making 007 the cinematic success story that he has become. Today, Bond is as popular as ever and his fans are eagerly awaiting the release of the next Bond film in 2002. *The World Is Not Enough* (1999) was one of the most successful of the Bond series; with it came a US and UK advance poster that has come to be known as the 'Flame Girl' design. Not only is it regarded as one of the very best Bond film posters, it is also considered to be one of the best poster designs for any film of the decade. Little wonder, then, that while Bond fans are anticipating the next Bond film, Bond poster collectors are keen to capture a glimpse of the next exciting poster campaign.

Tony Nourmand
July 2001

British 30 x 20 in (76 x 51 cm)
Style A

It was on seeing an image of a Beretta in his local library, that Joseph Caroff first visualised the 007 logo. This logo was commissioned by United Artists for press release letterheads for *Dr. No* and was subsequently used as part of the first campaign. By the time of the release of *From Russia With Love*, this image was so recognisable that it was used alone as the basis for this British poster.

HARRY SALTZMAN and
ALBERT R. BROCCOLI PRESENT
IAN FLEMING'S
THE FIRST JAM
DR. NO
TECHNICOLOR
STARRING
SEAN CONNERY
AS
007
AND
URSULA
ANDRESS
JOSEPH
WISEMAN
Screenplay by
RICHARD
MAIBAUM
JOHANNA
HARWOOD
AND
BERKELY
MATHER
Directed b

1962

Dr. No

On introducing James Bond in *Dr. No*, producers Albert R. Broccoli and Harry Saltzman could not have foreseen the phenomenon that the series of films would soon become. But the material already had a certain glamour. Here was an anti-hero who was terribly British, who killed in cold blood and yet was able to charm numerous beautiful women and solve the deadliest of crimes, all in a day's work.

This adaptation from the novel by Ian Fleming was one of the films most faithful to the original story. James Bond is sent to Jamaica with a mission: to investigate the mysterious circumstances surrounding the death of fellow agent John Strangways. The trail leads him to the island of Crab Key, the base of the SPECTRE headquarters of corrupt scientist Dr. No, whom Bond believes to be the murderer. Dr. No informs Bond of his aim of world domination and the destruction of the US space programme. Battle commences between Bond and Dr. No, until the villain finally falls into his own trap and dies.

Mitchell Hooks painted the iconic image of Sean Connery as Bond, with a smoking pistol in one hand and a cigarette in the other. This image was used internationally at the time, as well as in later poster campaigns. The posters featured Bond surrounded by several glamorous women, a visual shorthand that was to make the secret agent immediately recognizable to cinema audiences worldwide. Joseph Caroff designed the 007 logo, which, with a few variations, has been used throughout the series.

British 30 x 40 in (76 x 102 cm)
Artist/Illustrator Mitchell Hooks
Design David Chasman
Date of release October 1962

Japanese 58 x 20 in (147 x 51 cm)
Date of release May 1963
Translation: *007 Is The Killing Number*

Japanese 28 x 20 in (71 x 51 cm)
(Style A)

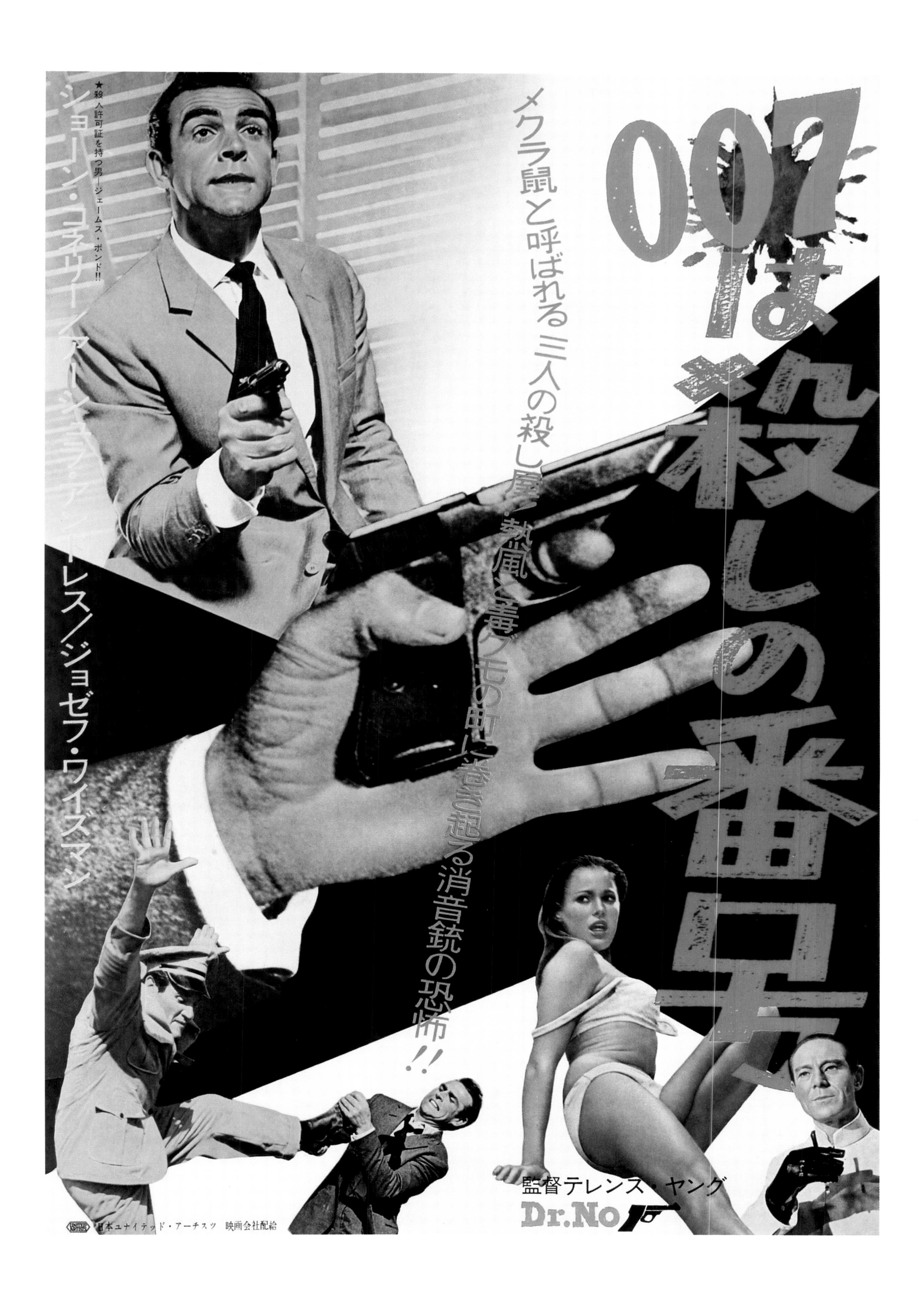
007は殺しの番号
メクラ鼠と呼ばれる三人の殺し屋・熱風と毒グモの町に巻き起る消音銃の恐怖!!
★殺人許可証を持つ男—ジェームス・ボンド!!
ショーン・コネリー／アーシュラ・アンドレス／ジョゼフ・ワイズマン
監督テレンス・ヤング
Dr.No
UNITED ARTISTS
日本ユナイテッド・アーチスツ　映画会社配給

Italian 28 x 13 in (71 x 33 cm)
Date of release January 1963
Translation: *Agent 007 Licence To Kill*

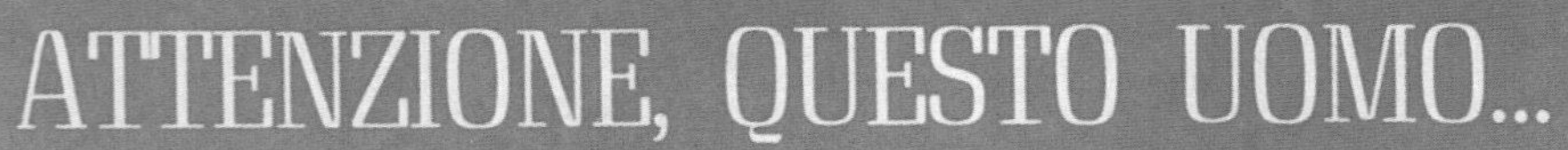

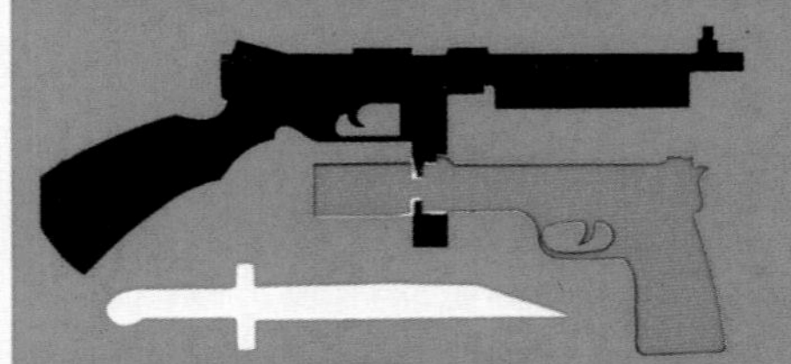

US 22 x 28 in (56 x 71 cm)
Design David Chasman
Date of release May 1963

German 33 x 46 in (84 x 117 cm)
Design/Illustrator Atelier Degen
Date of release January 1963
Translation: *James Bond Chases Dr. No*

JAMES BOND,
his code 007
The double "O" means he has a license to kill when he chooses... where he chooses... whom he chooses!
NOW HE IS A FLESH AND BLOOD EXPERIENCE ON THE SCREEN!
IAN FLEMING'S
Dr. No
THE FIRST JAMES BOND FILM ADVENTURE!
HARRY SALTZMAN and ALBERT R. BROCCOLI present IAN FLEMING'S Dr. No starring SEAN CONNERY as James Bond and URSULA ANDRESS
JOSEPH WISEMAN JACK LORD also starring BERNARD LEE Screenplay by RICHARD MAIBAUM, JOHANNA HARWOOD, and BERKLEY MATHER Directed by TERENCE YOUNG
Music Composed by MONTY NORMAN Produced by HARRY SALTZMAN and ALBERT R. BROCCOLI . . EON PRODUCTIONS, LTD. TECHNICOLOR Released thru UNITED UA ARTISTS
62/410

james bond 007 jagt dr. no - stop - james bond 007 jagt dr. no - stop
Harry Saltzman und Albert R. Broccoli zeigen
Ian Fleming's
JAMES BOND-007 JAGT DR. NO
UNITED ARTISTS
mit
Sean Connery
als James Bond
und Ursula Andress Joseph Wiseman
Jack Lord und Bernard Lee
Drehbuch: Richard Maibaum, Johanna Harwood und Berkley Mather
Regie: Terence Young Musik: Monty Norman
Produktion: Harry Saltzman und Albert R. Broccoli
Eon Productions, Ltd. Technicolor

DISTRIBUZIONE
HARRY SALTZMAN E ALBERT R. BROCCOLI presentano
UNITED ARTISTS
DEAR FILM
AGENTE 007
LICENZA DI UCCIDERE
DI IAN FLEMING
CON
E URSULA ANDRESS - JOSEPH WISEMAN
JACK LORD · BERNARD LEE
TECHNICOLOR
AVVERTENZA
ROTOLITO
SCENEGGIATURA DI
RICHARD MAIBAUM, JOHANNA HARWOOD E BERKLEY MATHER
REGIA DI
TERENCE YOUNG
MUSICHE COMPOSTE DA
MONTY NORMAN
PRODOTTO DA
HARRY SALTZMAN E ALBERT R. BROCCOLI UNA EON PRODUCTIONS, LTD

Italian 79 x 55 in (201 x 140 cm)
Artist/Illustrator Averardo Ciriello

French 31 x 16 in (79 x 41 cm)
Artist/Illustrator Boris Grinsson
Date of release March 1963
Translation: *James Bond Versus Dr. No*

This is the only illustration from the poster campaign which depicts the classic image of Sean Connery standing with Ursula Andress.

Danish 33 x 25 in (84 x 63 cm)
Date of release April 1963
Translation: *Agent 007 Mission: Kill Dr. No*

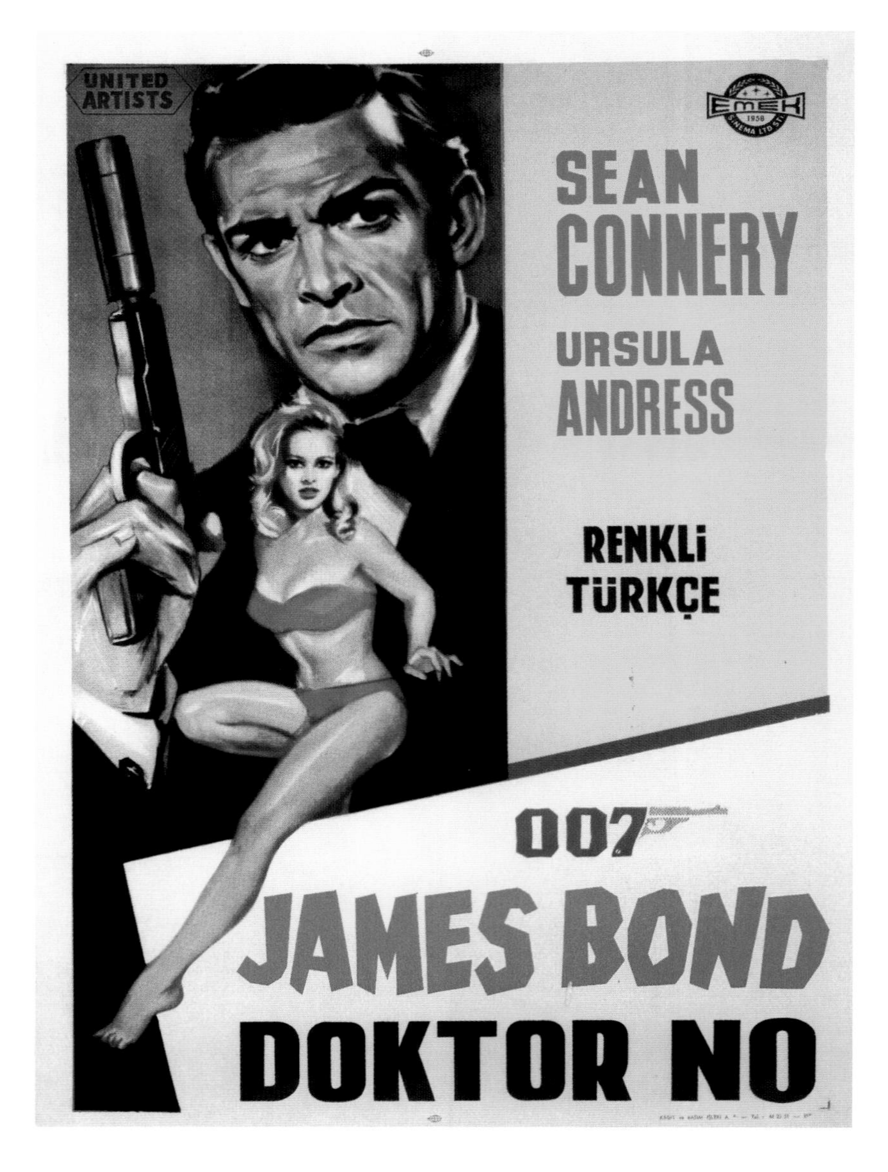

Turkish 40 x 28 in (100 x 72 cm)
Year of release 1966

Spanish 39 x 27 in (99 x 69 cm)
Artist/Illustrator Macario Gomez (Mac)
Date of release April 1963
Translation: *Agent 007 Versus The Satanic Dr. No*

HARRY SALTZMAN y ALBERT R. BROCCOLI
presentan la producción de IAN FLEMING
agente 007 contra el doctor NO
mac.
Interpretada por
SEAN CONNERY
en el papel de James Bond
Interpretada tambien por
URSULA ANDRESS • JOSEPH WISEMAN • JACK LORD • BERNARD LEE
Guión de RICHARD MAIBAUM, JOHANNA HARWOOD y BERKLEY MATHER • Dirigida por: TERENCE YOUNG
MUSICA COMPUESTA POR MONTY NORMAN • PRODUCIDA POR HARRY SALTZMAN y ALBERT R. BROCCOLI - EON PRODUCTIONS, LTD
CB films
UNITED ARTISTS
TECHNICOLOR (R)
Depósito Legal B. 4677 - 1963
I. G. MARÍ, S. A. - Barcelona

US 27 x 14 in (69 x 36 cm)
(Benton Co.)

This is the alternative US 22 x 14 inch poster, also known as the US window card, which was designed and printed for use in the deep South and promotes the black actor, John Kitzmiller.

French 63 x 47 in (160 x 119 cm)
(Pink Strip)
Artist/Illustrator Boris Grinsson

HARRY SALTZMAN et
ALBERT R. BROCCOLI
présentent
JAMES
BOND
007
CONTRE
Dr. NO
(Dr. NO)
d'après le livre de IAN FLEMING: "Dr. NO"
avec SEAN CONNERY
DANS LE RÔLE DE JAMES BOND
et URSULA ANDRESS JOSEPH WISEMAN
JACK LORD et BERNARD LEE
Scénario de RICHARD MAIBAUM et JOHANNA HARWOOD
Réalisé par TERENCE YOUNG
Musique composée et dirigée par MONTY NORMAN
Produit par HARRY SALTZMAN et ALBERT R. BROCCOLI
EON PRODUCTIONS LTD
UNITED ARTISTS
TECHNICOLOR
distribué par Les Artistes Associés

1963
From Russia With Love

Following the huge success of *Dr. No*, the much anticipated follow-up film had to be equally exciting and impressive. President J. F. Kennedy had named *From Russia With Love* as one of his top ten books, so Broccoli and Saltzman were in good company when they chose this novel as the basis for the next Bond film. With a greatly increased budget, this film was significant as their last to show Bond as an ordinary detective relying more on his human instincts than the gadgetry that was to become the hallmark of the later Bond films.

James Bond flies to Istanbul with instructions from MI6 to steal an important cypher machine called the Lektor. M informs Bond that a defected Soviet agent named Tatiana is in love with him and so wishes to help. Bond is suspicious, but Tatiana is unaware that her superior, Colonel Rosa Klebb, is working for SPECTRE, the organization seeking revenge for the death of Dr. No.

The British campaign utilized the now famous Sean Connery pose by Eric Pulford, which became synonymous with Bond. While the European posters had a more traditional painterly style, the American campaign devised by David Chasman took a more modern and innovative approach, using mainly photomontage and catchy tag lines.

British 30 x 40 in (76 x 102 cm)
Artist/Illustrator Renato Fratini & Eric Pulford
Date of release October 1963

JAMES BOND
IS BACK!
HARRY SALTZMAN & ALBERT R. BROCCOLI present IAN FLEMING'S
FROM RUSSIA WITH LOVE
A
TECHNICOLOR®
Renato Fratini
TITLE SONG WRITTEN BY Lionel BART
PRODUCED BY HARRY SALTZMAN AND ALBERT R. BROCCOLI
DIRECTED BY TERENCE YOUNG
EON PRODUCTIONS LTD.

UNITED ARTISTS

Japanese 58 x 20 in (147 x 51 cm)
Date of release April 1964
Translation: *007 at a critical moment*

Japanese 59 x 37 in (150 x 93 cm)

襲いくる罠…罠… 全世界の暗殺者に単身挑む007必殺の消音銃!!
007
007
007
007
ジェームズ・ボンド
「007」シリーズ第2弾!!
主演 ショーン・コネリー
監督 テレンス・ヤング
原作 イアン・フレミング
FROM RUSSIA WITH LOVE
〈総天然色〉
007
危機一発
ダニエラ・ビアンキ/ペドロ・アルメンダリス/脚色リチャード・メイバウム/撮影テッド・ムーア
主題歌「ロシアより愛をこめて」オデオンレコード/ロンドンレコード/パイレコード/グローブレコード/日本版キングレコード〈紀本ヨシオ〉
主題曲「007のテーマ」ユナイトレコード/原作「ロシアより愛をこめて」創元推理文庫/ユナイト映画配給
UNITED ARTISTS

US 22 x 28 in (86 x 71 cm)
Design David Chasman
Date of release April 1964

US 41 x 27 in (104 x 69 cm)
(Style A)
Design David Chasman

US 81 x 41 in (206 x 104 cm)
(Style A)
Design David Chasman

69,000,007 JAMES BOND FANS LIVE IN A THROBBING WORLD OF HOT-BLOODED EXCITEMENT!

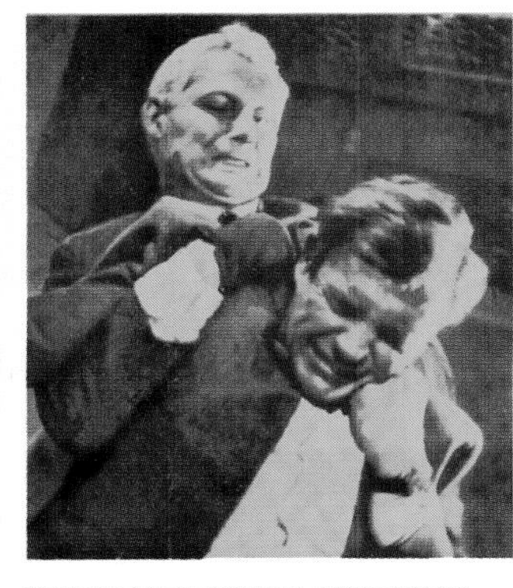

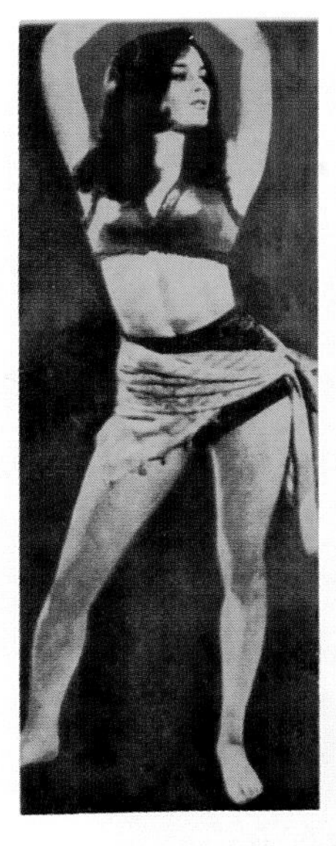

DON'T YOU THINK IT'S TIME
YOU MET SECRET AGENT 007?
NOW HIS INCREDIBLE WOMEN...
HIS INCREDIBLE ENEMIES...
HIS INCREDIBLE NEW
ADVENTURES
EXPLODE ON THE SCREEN!!!

HARRY SALTZMAN AND ALBERT R. BROCCOLI PRESENT
IAN FLEMING'S

FROM RUSSIA WITH LOVE

STARRING
SEAN CONNERY AS JAMES BOND

Also starring
PEDRO ARMENDARIZ LOTTE LENYA
ROBERT SHAW BERNARD LEE AS "M"
And introducing DANIELA BIANCHI

Screenplay by RICHARD MAIBAUM Adapted by JOHANNA HARWOOD Title Song Written by LIONEL BART Orchestral Music Composed and Conducted by JOHN BARRY

Produced by HARRY SALTZMAN AND ALBERT R. BROCCOLI Directed by TERENCE YOUNG

TECHNICOLOR® EON PRODUCTIONS LTD. Released thru UNITED ARTISTS

US set of 4 door panels, each 60 x 20 in
(152 x 51 cm)
Design David Chasman

A set of four door panels was first introduced in the advertising campaign for *From Russia With Love*, and were subsequently used for the following three Bond films. They were printed in small quantities and used only at the premiere for each film. Due to their rarity and strikingly bold images, they are now highly prized by poster collectors.

IS
FROM RUSSIA WITH LOVE
Released thru UNITED ARTISTS
TECHNICOLOR
FROM RUSSIA WITH LOVE 3 64-35

BACK!
HARRY SALTZMAN AND ALBERT R. BROCCOLI PRESENT IAN FLEMING'S
FROM RUSSIA WITH LOVE
starring
SEAN CONNERY AS JAMES BOND
Also starring PEDRO ARMENDARIZ LOTTE LENYA ROBERT SHAW BERNARD LEE as "M"
And introducing DANIELA BIANCHI
Screenplay by RICHARD MAIBAUM
Adapted by JOHANNA HARWOOD
Title Song Written by LIONEL BART
Orchestral Music Composed and Conducted by JOHN BARRY
Produced by HARRY SALTZMAN AND ALBERT R. BROCCOLI
Directed by TERENCE YOUNG
EON PRODUCTIONS LTD
TECHNICOLOR
Released thru UNITED ARTISTS
FROM RUSSIA WITH LOVE 4 64-35

Italian 55 x 39 in (140 x 99 cm)
Artist/Illustrator Averardo Ciriello
Date of release January 1964
Translation: *To 007, From Russia With Love*

French 31 x 24 in (79 x 61 cm)
Artist/Illustrator Boris Grinsson
Date of release March 1964
Translation: *Hearty Kisses From Russia*

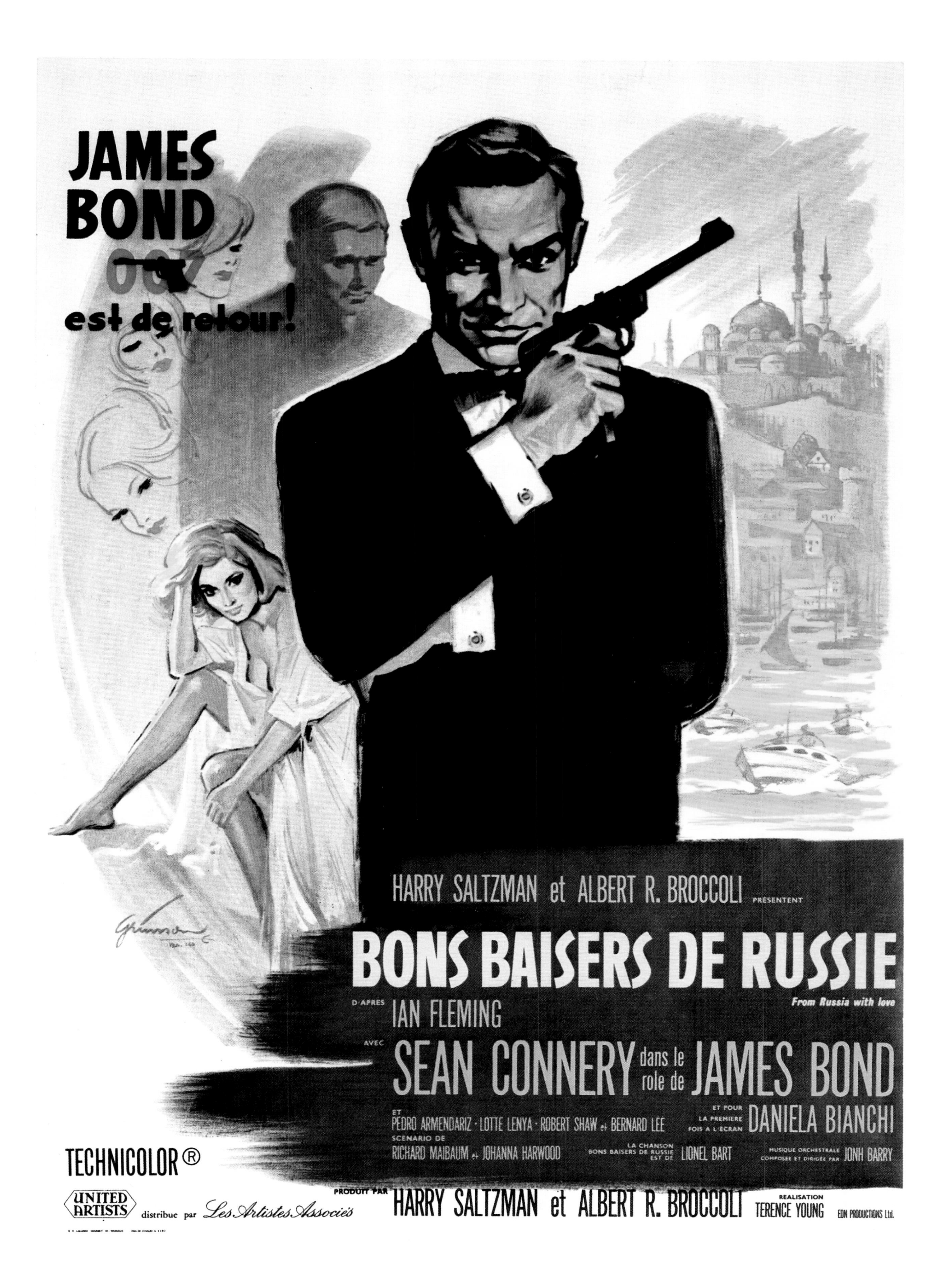
JAMES
BOND
007
est de retour!
HARRY SALTZMAN et ALBERT R. BROCCOLI PRÉSENTENT
BONS BAISERS DE RUSSIE
From Russia with love
D'APRES IAN FLEMING
AVEC SEAN CONNERY dans le role de JAMES BOND
ET PEDRO ARMENDARIZ · LOTTE LENYA · ROBERT SHAW et BERNARD LÉE
ET POUR LA PREMIERE FOIS A L'ECRAN DANIELA BIANCHI
SCENARIO DE RICHARD MAIBAUM et JOHANNA HARWOOD
LA CHANSON BONS BAISERS DE RUSSIE EST DE LIONEL BART
MUSIQUE ORCHESTRALE COMPOSÉE ET DIRIGÉE PAR JONH BARRY
TECHNICOLOR®
UNITED ARTISTS distribue par Les Artistes Associés
PRODUIT PAR HARRY SALTZMAN et ALBERT R. BROCCOLI
REALISATION TERENCE YOUNG
EON PRODUCTIONS Ltd.

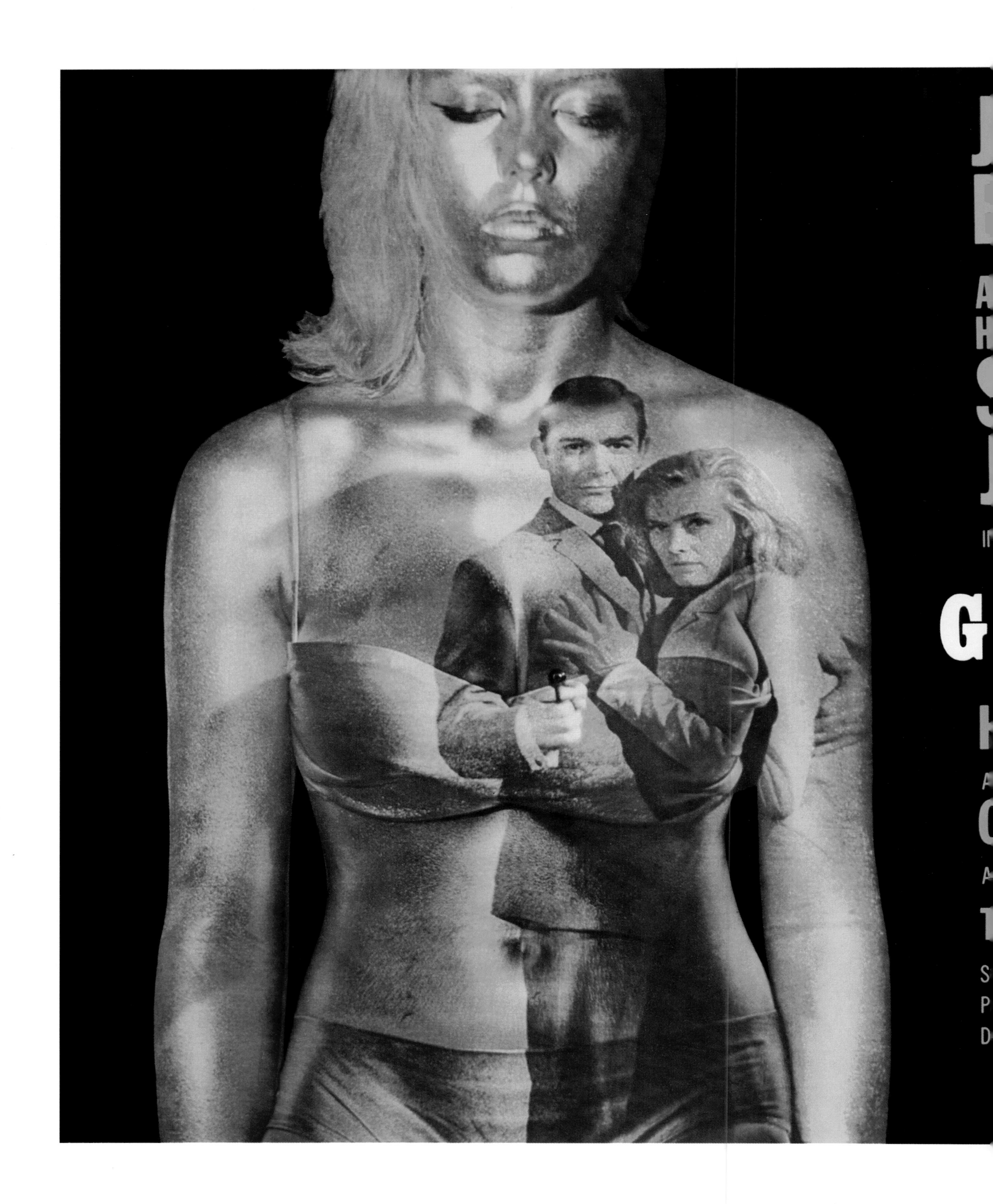

1964

Goldfinger

With Guy Hamilton directing his first Bond film, *Goldfinger* marked a change of direction and an artistic peak of the Bond series. Bond's character became more tongue-in-cheek, and was able to remain remarkably cool and collected in the toughest of situations. This was the first Bond film to be labelled a box-office blockbuster, and it received an unprecedented reception from audiences around the world.

Bond's task is to investigate Auric Goldfinger, who is suspected by the Bank of England of smuggling gold in and out of the country. He seduces Goldfinger's confederate Jill Masterson, who is then very willing to help him discover the truth behind Goldfinger's grand scheme. As a horrific warning to Bond, Jill is killed by Goldfinger who paints her from head to toe in gold paint. Bond then encounters Pussy Galore, who is equally enthusiastic about assisting the ever-charming detective.

Robert Brownjohn designed the British posters, and many of the main elements were taken directly from the distinctive title sequence for which he was also responsible. Brownjohn also collaborated with David Chasman on the American campaign, which resulted for the first time in American posters being bold and colourful, most notably the US set of 4 60 x 20 inch posters, also known as door panels.

British 30 x 40 in (76 x 102 cm)
(Style A)
Design Robert Brownjohn
Date of release September 1964

British 30 x 40 in (76 x 102 cm)
(Style B)
Design Robert Brownjohn

This more conservative design for the British 30 x 40 inch poster, also known as the Quad, was designed to be used mainly in Ireland. The publicity department responsible for the campaign had noticed that exposed body parts tended to be painted over by sensitive individuals. Therefore, a hand has replaced the provocative golden body image.

US 41 x 27 in (104 x 69 cm)
Design David Chasman &
Robert Brownjohn
Date of release December 1964

US 36 x 14 in (91 x 36 cm)
Design David Chasman
& Robert Brownjohn

JAMES BOND IS BACK IN ACTION!
EVERYTHING HE TOUCHES
TURNS TO EXCITEMENT!!!
ALBERT R. BROCCOLI and HARRY SALTZMAN present
SEAN CONNERY AS AGENT 007
in IAN FLEMING'S
"GOLDFINGER"
STARRING
GERT FROBE as GOLDFINGER
HONOR BLACKMAN as PUSSY GALORE
ALSO STARRING SHIRLEY EATON
SCREENPLAY BY RICHARD MAIBAUM and PAUL DEHN
PRODUCED BY HARRY SALTZMAN and ALBERT R. BROCCOLI
DIRECTED BY GUY HAMILTON
TECHNICOLOR®
RELEASED THRU UNITED ARTISTS
Exciting original motion picture soundtrack album available on United Artists Records.
Copyright © 1964 United Artists Corporation. Printed in U.S.A.

US set of 4 door panels, each 60 x 20 in (152 x 51 cm)
Design David Chasman & Robert Brownjohn

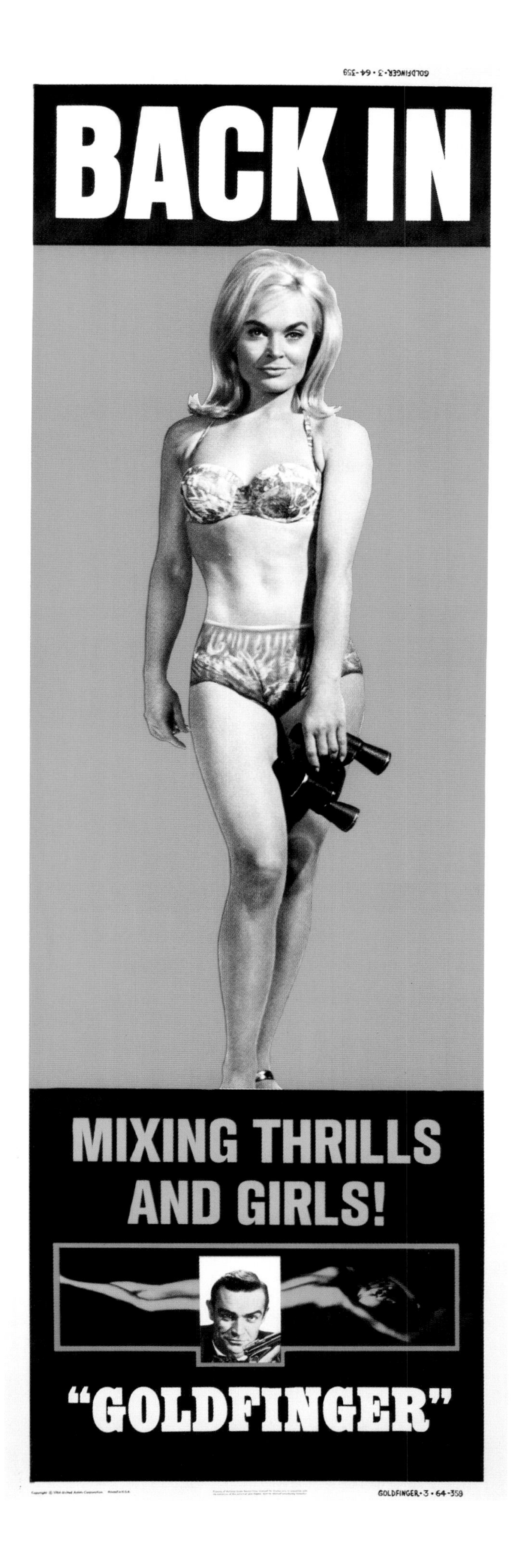
BACK IN
MIXING THRILLS
AND GIRLS!
"GOLDFINGER"
GOLDFINGER-3-64-358

ACTION!
MIXING DANGER
AND GIRLS!
"GOLDFINGER"
GOLDFINGER-4-64-358

Japanese 58 x 20 in (147 x 51 cm)
Date of release April 1965

Japanese 28 x 20 in (71 x 51 cm)

ショーン・コネリー／
オナー・ブラックマン■ゲルト・フレーベ■監督ガイ・ハミルトン
シャーリー・イートン■タニア・マレット■音楽モンティー・ノーマン
●全世界アクション・ファンの拍手を浴びて最大の危機に挑む― 颯爽ジェームズ・ボンド！
ジェームズ・ボンドシリーズ第3作
総天然色
007
ゴールドフィンガー
SEAN CONNERY
in IAN FLEMING'S as AGENT 007 "GOLDFINGER"
原作イアン・フレミング《早川書房刊》

Swedish 39 x 28 in (99 x 71 cm)
Artist/Illustrator Gosta Aberg
Date of release February 1965

Italian 28 x 13 in (71 x 33 cm)
Date of release January 1965
Translation: *Agent 007, Mission Goldfinger*

French 63 x 47 in (160 x 119 cm)
Artist/Illustrator Jean Mascii
Date of release February 1965

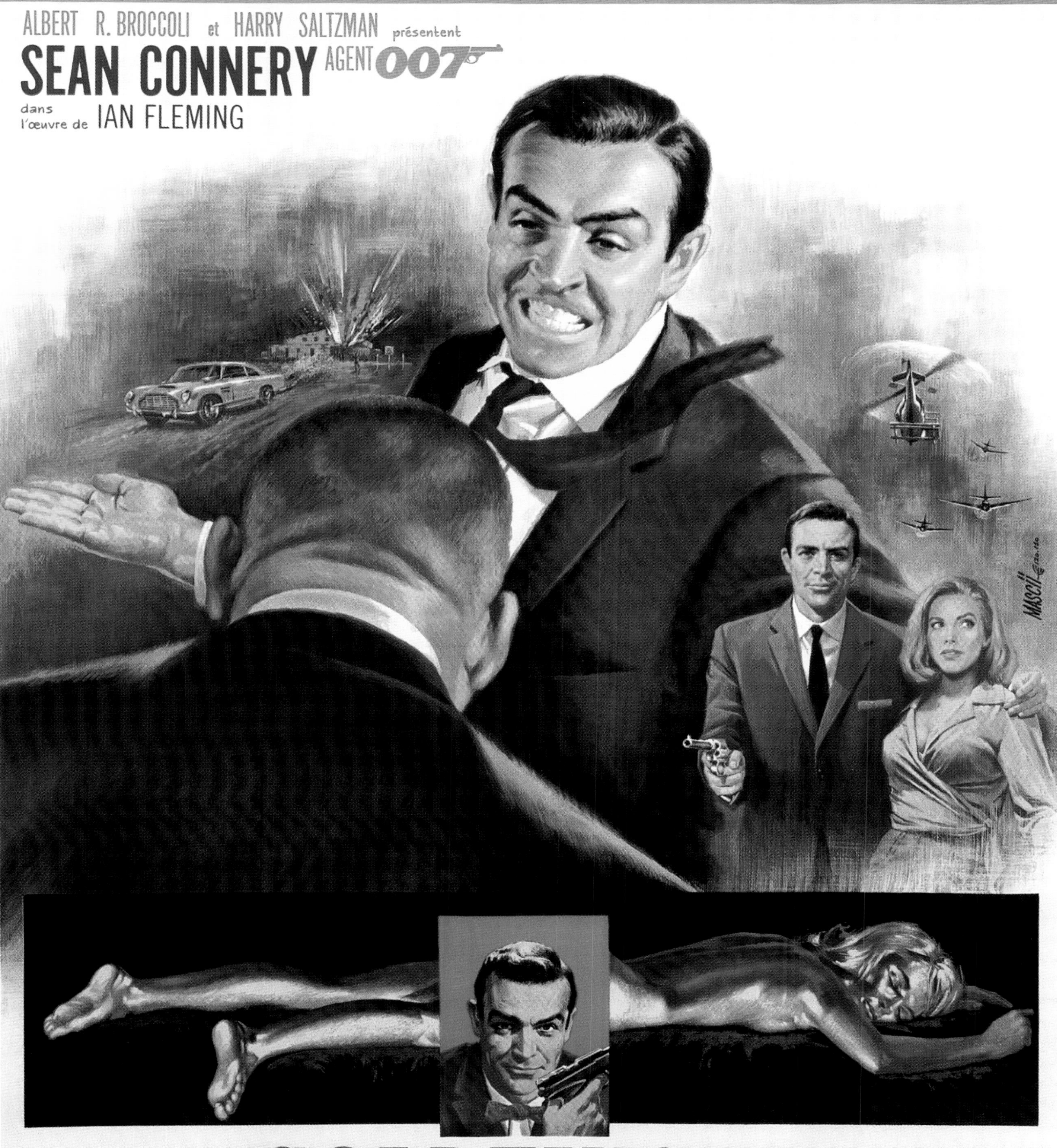
JAMES BOND DE NOUVEAU EN ACTION!
ALBERT R. BROCCOLI et HARRY SALTZMAN présentent
SEAN CONNERY AGENT 007
dans l'œuvre de IAN FLEMING
MASCII
GOLDFINGER
avec GERT FROBE dans le rôle de GOLDFINGER
HONOR BLACKMAN dans le rôle de PUSSY GALORE
et avec SHIRLEY EATON
TECHNICOLOR®
Scénario RICHARD MAIBAUM et PAUL DEHN
Produit par HARRY SALTZMAN et ALBERT R. BROCCOLI
Mise en scène de GUY HAMILTON
distribué par Les Artistes Associés
UNITED ARTISTS

1965

Thunderball

This film became the centre of a complicated legal battle when former Ian Fleming associates Kevin McClory and Jack Whittingham claimed Fleming had based the novel *Thunderball* on elements of a screenplay created years before. Eventually, an agreement was made and the fanatical public were more than satisfied with the film. Another box-office smash, *Thunderball* proved that Bond mania had finally hit the world.

SPECTRE hijacks two atomic bombs from a British Vulcan aircraft. The Prime Minister is then given an ultimatum: either SPECTRE will destroy a major city in Britain or America, or the British Government must pay them a fortune in ransom. Bond has to race against time and is sent to the Bahamas to track down the warheads. He discovers that an underwater operation has been organizing the transportation of the bombs to Miami, the target.

The publicity campaign instructed audiences to 'Look Up! Look Down! Look Out! Here Comes The Biggest Bond Of All!' The highly successful creative partnership of Robert McGinnis and Frank McCarthy was introduced for this campaign, each using his specialist artistic skills with such ability that their designs were used worldwide. Noted Italian artist Averardo Ciriello produced a controversial image for the Italian market of Sean Connery without shorts, based on an unused McGinnis concept. The artwork was eventually used, but adapted with the addition of a modicum of clothing.

British 30 x 40 in (76 x 102 cm)
Artist/Illustrator Robert McGinnis
Date of release December 1965

HERE COMES
THE BIGGEST
BOND OF ALL!
EAN CONNERY in IAN FLEMING'S
NDERBALL"
A
UNITED ARTISTS
R · ADOLFO CELI · LUCIANA PALUZZI · RIK VAN NUTTER
ed by TERENCE YOUNG
PANAVISION® TECHNICOLOR®
Based on the original story by KEVIN McCLORY, JACK WHITTINGHAM and IAN FLEMING

LOOK UP!

LOOK DOWN!

LOOK OUT!

HERE COMES THE BIGGEST BOND OF ALL!

ALBERT R. BROCCOLI and HARRY SALTZMAN present

SEAN CONNERY

in IAN FLEMING'S "THUNDERBALL"

CLAUDINE AUGER · ADOLFO CELI
LUCIANA PALUZZI Produced by KEVIN McCLORY Directed by TERENCE YOUNG Screenplay by RICHARD MAIBAUM and JOHN HOPKINS
Based on an original story by KEVIN McCLORY, JACK WHITTINGHAM and IAN FLEMING PANAVISION® TECHNICOLOR® Released thru UNITED ARTISTS

US 41 x 27 in (104 x 69 cm)
Artist/Illustrator Robert McGinnis & Frank McCarthy
Date of release December 1965

Danish 33 x 23 in (84 x 58 cm)
Featuring artwork by Robert McGinnis
Date of release December 1965
Translation: *Agent 007 Into The Fire*

SEAN CONNERY
AGENT 007 i ILDEN
ALBERT R. BROCCOLI HARRY SALTZMAN
præsenterer
IAN FLEMING'S
"THUNDERBALL"
CLAUDINE AUGER · ADOLFO CELI · LUCIANA PALUZZI
PANAVISION
TECHNICOLOR
KEVIN McCLORY
TERENCE YOUNG
RICHARD MAIBAUM JOHN HOPKINS
KEVIN McCLORY JACK WHITTINGHAM IAN FLEMING'S

UNITED
ARTISTS

US set of 4 door panels, each 60 x 20 in (152 x 51 cm)

THUNDERBALL 65-372 #3
LOO7K
OUT!
THUNDERBALL 65-372 #3

HERE COMES
THE BIGGEST
BOND OF ALL!
ALBERT R. BROCCOLI
and HARRY SALTZMAN present
SEAN CONNERY
in IAN FLEMING'S
"THUNDERBALL"
CLAUDINE AUGER · ADOLFO CELI
LUCIANA PALUZZI
Produced by KEVIN McCLORY · Directed by TERENCE YOUNG · Screenplay by RICHARD MAIBAUM
and JOHN HOPKINS
Based on an original story by KEVIN McCLORY, JACK WHITTINGHAM and IAN FLEMING
PANAVISION® TECHNICOLOR®
Released thru UNITED ARTISTS
THUNDERBALL 65-372 #4

Japanese 58 x 20 in (147 x 51 cm)
Featuring art by Frank McCarthy
Date of release December 1965
Translation: *Thunderball Fighting*

Italian 79 x 55 in (201 x 140 cm)
(Advance)
Artist/Illustrator Averardo Ciriello
Date of release December 1965
Translation: *Operation Thunderball*

007

SEAN CONNERY
as JAMES BOND in

British 39 x 59 in (99 x 150 cm)
(Special Premiere poster)

Thunderball

1967
Casino Royale

Screen rights to *Casino Royale*, Fleming's first Bond novel, were originally owned by Charles K. Feldman. He opted to adapt the novel into a spy spoof, a parody of the Bond films of the sixties and a big-budget madcap comedy. Despite the endless supply of innuendos, general goofiness and lack of serious plot, the film succeeded in entertaining the masses and was a modest box-office success. It also had an amazing array of successful actors involved, including David Niven, Ursula Andress, Orson Welles and Woody Allen.

A happily retired James Bond is called back to serve on Her Majesty's Secret Service, following the death of M. Many international spies have been killed recently, and the British, Soviet, French and American governments have chosen to work together to combat the organization suspected of being responsible for the murders – SMERSH. In an attempt to confuse the opposition, all of the agents are re-named James Bond. And, as usual, the real Bond is assisted by numerous attractive young ladies.

Feldman hired James Bond illustrator Robert McGinnis to create the central image of the psychedelic girl, which was used internationally. For the US campaign, a set of six door panels was produced in keeping with those that were being used by Eon Productions at the time. For the Italian campaign, Giorgio Olivetti created three special posters, each introducing one of the three James Bond wannabes and fabulous Bond girls.

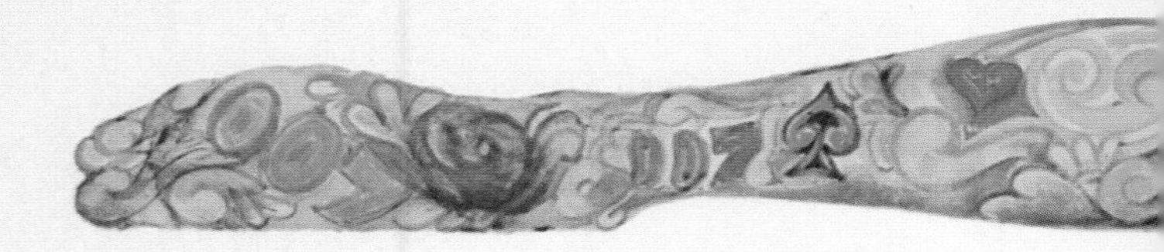

CHARLES K. FELDM
CASIN
ROYAL
IS TOO MU
FOR ONE
JAMES BON
Produced by CHARLES K. FELDMAN and JERRY BRESLER Directed by JOHN HUSTON, KEN HUGHES,
Copyright © 1967 by Columbia Pictures Corporation. All Rights Reserved. PRINTED IN U.S.A.

US 22 x 28 in (56 x 71 cm)
Artist/Illustrator Robert McGinnis
Date of release April 1967

CHARLES K. FELDMAN
presents
A FAMOUS ARTISTS PRODUCTION LTD.
CASINO ROYALE
Starring
PETER SELLERS
URSULA ANDRESS
DAVID NIVEN
WOODY ALLEN
JOANNA PETTET
ORSON WELLES
DALIAH LAVI
Guest Stars
DEBORAH KERR
WILLIAM HOLDEN
CHARLES BOYER
JEAN-PAUL BELMONDO
GEORGE RAFT
JOHN HUSTON
and Co-Starring
TERENCE COOPER
BARBARA BOUCHET
With
GABRIELLA LICUDI
TRACY REED
TRACEY CRISP
KURT KASZNAR
ELAINE TAYLOR
ANGELA SCOULAR
plus a Bondwagon full of the most
beautiful and talented girls you ever saw!
JAMES
BOND
007
CASINO ROYALE
ERT PARRISH, JOE McGRATH Screenplay by WOLF MANKOWITZ, JOHN LAW, MICHAEL SAYERS Suggested by the Ian Fleming novel Music by BURT BACHARACH PANAVISION® TECHNICOLOR® A COLUMBIA PICTURES RELEASE
Property of National Screen Service Corp. Licensed for display only in connection with the exhibition of this picture at your theatre. Must be returned immediately thereafter.
67/72

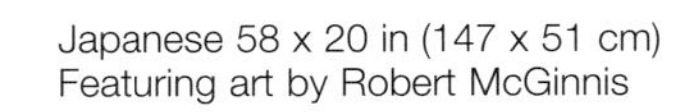

Japanese 58 x 20 in (147 x 51 cm)
Featuring art by Robert McGinnis

Japanese 28 x 20 in (71 x 51 cm)
Featuring art by Robert McGinnis

まったく新しい、ぜいたくな、最高におもしろいボンド映画の誕生！
007
カジノ・ロワイヤル
ピーター・セラーズ ★ アーシュラ・アンドレス
デビッド・ニブン ★ ウディ・アレン
ジョアンナ・プティット ★ オーソン・ウェルズ
ダリア・ラビ
デボラ・カー ★ ウィリアム・ホールデン
シャルル・ボワイエ ★ ジョージ・ラフト
ジョン・ヒューストン
テレンス・クーパー ★ バーバラ・ブーシェ
JAMES BOND 007
CASINO ROYALE
《パナビジョン・テクニカラー作品》
製作■チャールズ・K・フェルドマン ／ ジェリー・ブレスラー
監督■ジョン・ヒューストン ／ ケン・ヒューズ ／ バル・ゲスト
ロバート・パリッシュ ／ ジョー・マッグラス
音楽■バート・バカラック
演奏■ハーブ・アルパートとティファナ・ブラス
提供■コロムビア映画
COLUMBIA PICTURES
映倫
42253

Italian set of 3 each 79 x 55 in
(201 x 140 cm)
Artist/Illustrator Giorgio Olivetti

COLUMBIA
CEIAD
DAVID NIVEN
è
JAMES BOND 007
CASINO ROYALE
UNA PRODUZIONE CHARLES K.FELDMAN

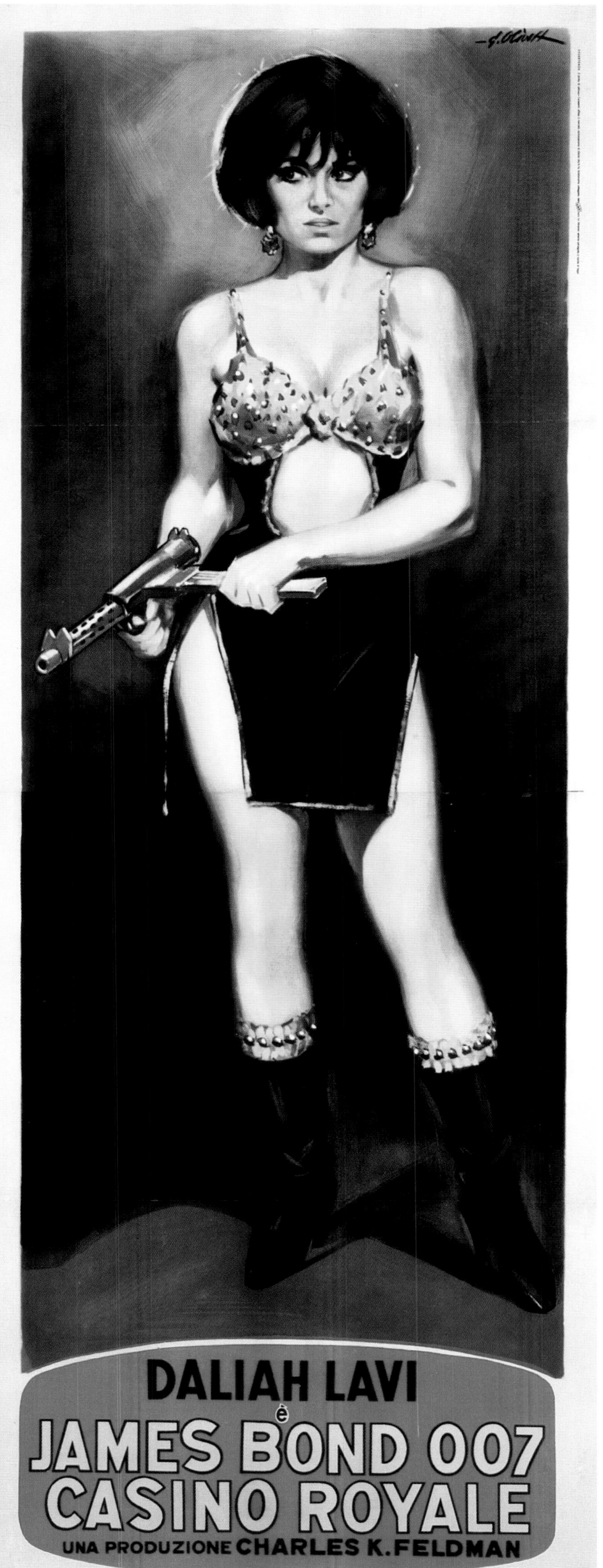
DALIAH LAVI
è
JAMES BOND 007
CASINO ROYALE
UNA PRODUZIONE CHARLES K.FELDMAN
Prima Edizione Italiana Anno 1967

US set of 6 door panels, each 60 x 20 in
(152 x 51 cm)

CHARLES K. FELDMAN'S
CASINO ROYALE
IS *TOO MUCH*
FOR ONE JAMES BOND
A COLUMBIA PICTURES RELEASE

CHARLES K. FELDMAN'S
CASINO ROYALE
IS *TOO MUCH*
FOR ONE JAMES BOND
A COLUMBIA PICTURES RELEASE

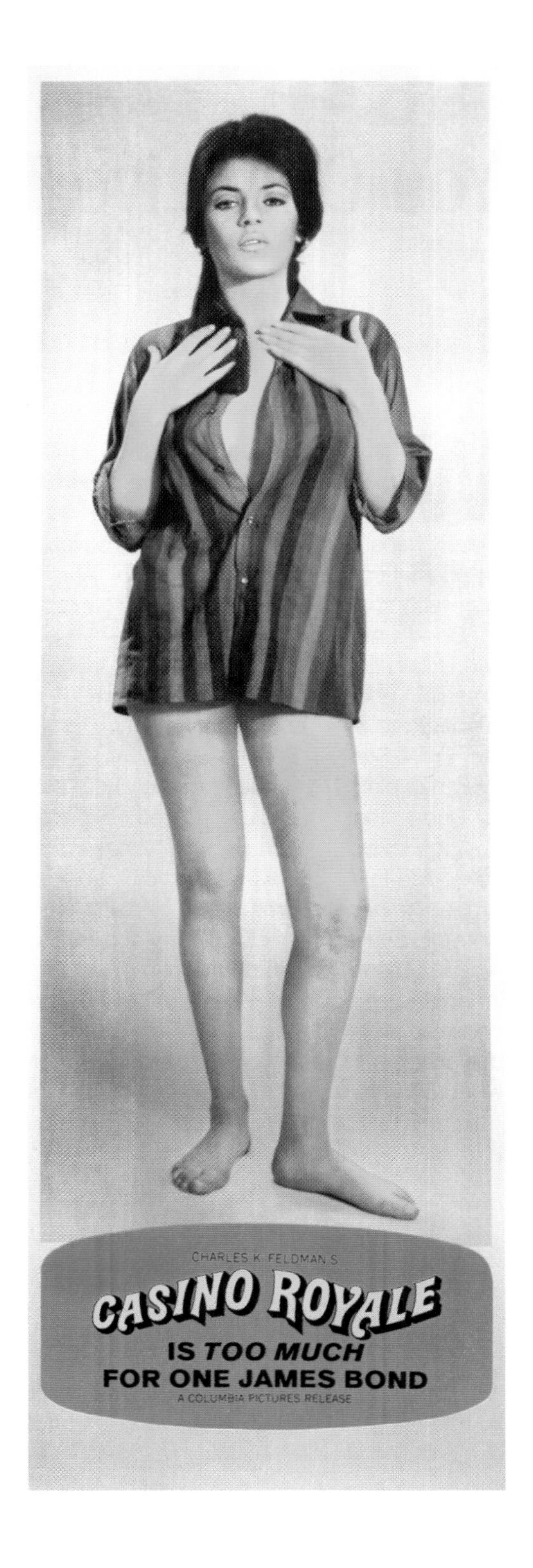
CHARLES K. FELDMAN'S
CASINO ROYALE
IS *TOO MUCH*
FOR ONE JAMES BOND
A COLUMBIA PICTURES RELEASE

British 30 x 40 in (76 x 102 cm)
(Style A)
Artist/Illustrator Frank McCarthy

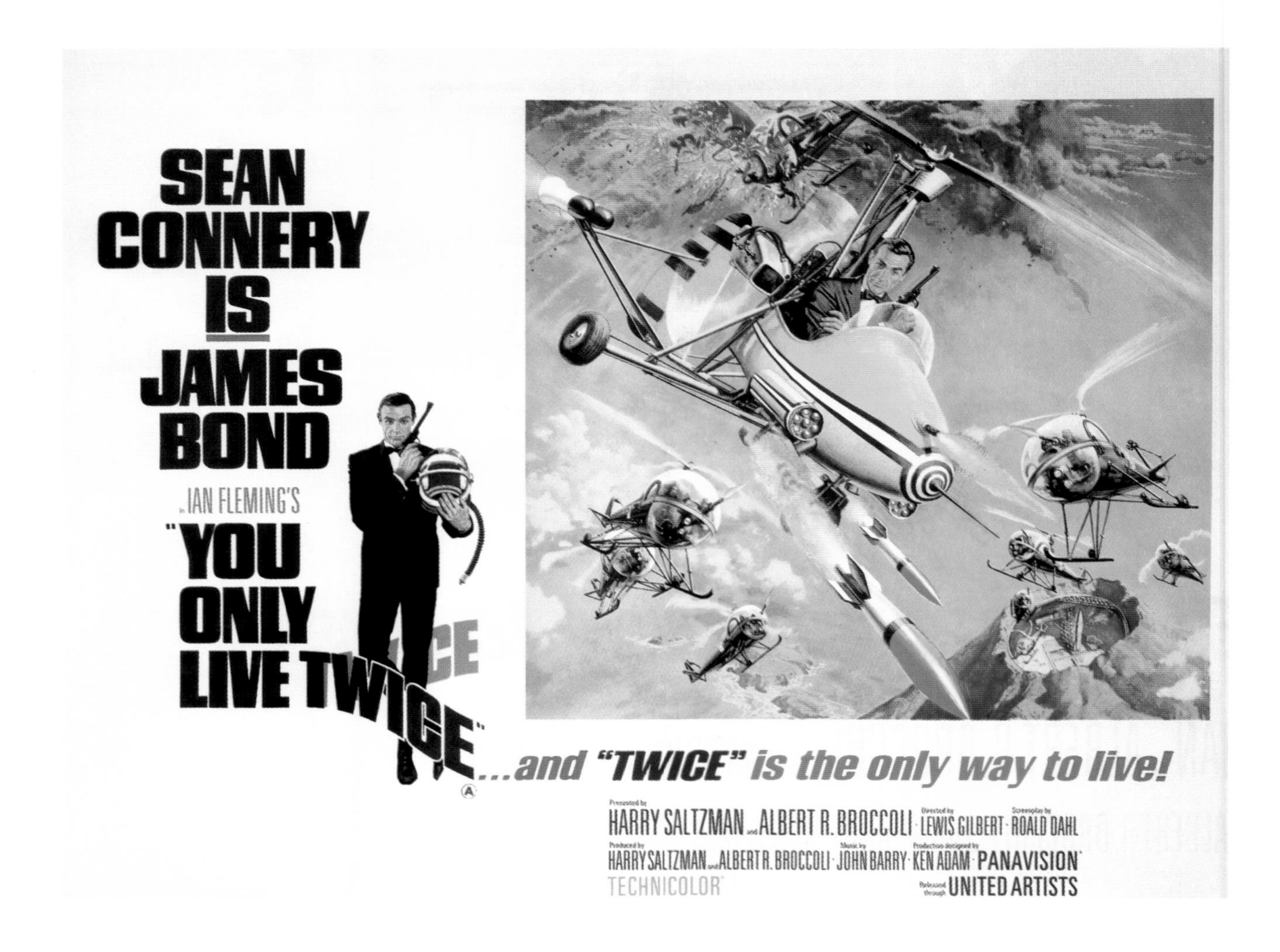

British 30 x 40 in (76 x 102 cm)
(Style B)
Artist/Illustrator Frank McCarthy

US 41 x 27 in (104 x 69 cm)
(Advance)
Date of release June 1967

THIS MAN IS JAMES BOND

FIRST

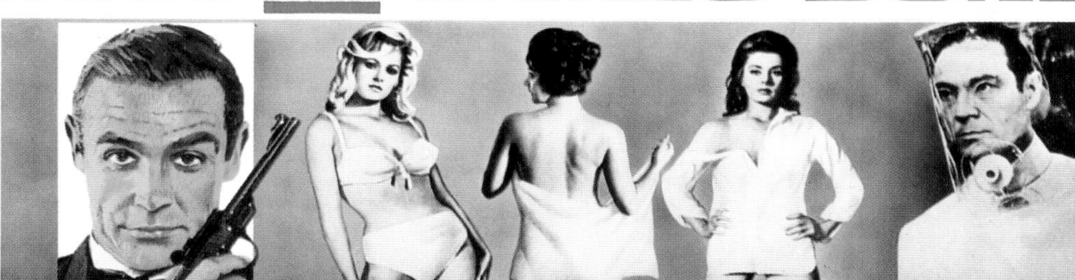

THEN

NEXT

LAST

IN IAN FLEMING'S

"YOU ONLY LIVE TWICE"

COMING!

67/225

US set of 4 door panels, each 60 x 20 in
(152 x 51 cm)

IS JAMES
LIVE
Music by
Production designed by
HARRY SALTZMAN · JOHN BARRY · KEN ADAM

BOND!
TWICE
TWICE"
Released thru
PANAVISION® TECHNICOLOR® UNITED ARTISTS

Japanese 58 x 20 in (147 x 51 cm)
Date of release June 1967
Translation: *007 Dies Twice*

Italian 39 x 27 in (99 x 69 cm)
Artist/Illustrator Robert McGinnis
Date of release October 1967

SEAN
CONNERY
E'
JAMES
BOND
IN AGENTE
007
SI VIVE
SOLO
DUE VOLTE
DEAR FILM
UNITED ARTISTS
Transamerica
Vecchioni & Guadagno, Via del Casale de Merode, 8 · Roma · Agosto 1967
Printed in Italy
PRIMA EDIZIONE ITALIANA ANNO MCMLXVII
AVVERTENZA

French 31 x 24 in (79 x 61 cm)
Date of release December 1969
Translation: *The Secret Service Of Her Majesty*

French 126 x 43 in (320 x 109 cm)
Artist/Illustrator Yves Thos

JAMES BOND
007
est de retour
AU SERVICE
SECRET
DE SA MAJESTE
"ON HER MAJESTY'S
SECRET SERVICE"

Italian 79 x 55 in (201 x 140 cm)
(Advance)
Date of release December 1969

US 41 x 27 in (104 x 69 cm)
Style A
Date of release December 1969

JAMES
BOND
007
IS
BACK!

ALBERT R. BROCCOLI and HARRY SALTZMAN
present
JAMES BOND 007
in IAN FLEMING'S
"ON HER MAJESTY'S
SECRET SERVICE"

starring GEORGE LAZENBY · DIANA RIGG · TELLY SAVALAS as Blofeld
also starring GABRIELE FERZETTI and ILSE STEPPAT Produced by ALBERT R. BROCCOLI and HARRY SALTZMAN
Directed by PETER HUNT · Screenplay by RICHARD MAIBAUM · Music by JOHN BARRY · PANAVISION® · TECHNICOLOR®

United Artists
Entertainment from
Transamerica Corporation

A 70/9

Japanese 58 x 20 in (147 x 51 cm)
Featuring artwork by Robert McGinnis
& Frank McCarthy
Date of release December 1969
Translation: *The Queen's 007*

Japanese 28 x 20 in (71 x 51 cm)
(Style B)

シリーズ最高の面白さ！シリーズ最大のスケール！007＝ボンド・シリーズ第六弾！
スイス・アルプスの頂上からスキーで大脱出――――
ニュー・アストン・マーチンをとばしてヨーロッパ縦断の大追撃！
テクニカラー/パナビジョン
女王陛下の
007
HARRY SALTZMAN and ALBERT R. BROCCOLI
present
JAMES BOND 007
in IAN FLEMING'S
"ON HER MAJESTY'S SECRET SERVICE"
ジョージ・レーゼンビイ
ダイアナ・リグ
テリー・サバラス
ガブリエレ・フェルゼッティ
アンジェラ・スコーラー
バーナード・リー
ルイス・マクスウェル
デズモンド・ルウェリン
■ボンド・ガールズ（11人の美女たち）
製作 ハリー・サルツマン
アルバート・R・ブロッコリ
監督ピーター・ハント
原作イアン・フレミング
主題歌ルイ・アームストロング
ユナイト映画
United Artists
映倫
44324

Set of 3 each 22 x 16 in
(56 x 41 cm)
(Unused artwork)

GEORGE LAZENBY- THE ANSWER TO MAIDENSPRAYERS

22 x 16 in (56 x 41 cm)
(Unused artwork)

30 x 20 in (76 x 51 cm)
(Unused artwork)

30 x 20 in (76 x 51 cm)
(Unused artwork)

THE NEW BOND
007 and Bride

ALBERT R. BROCCOLI and HARRY SALTZMAN present
JAMES BOND 007
in IAN FLEMING'S
"ON HER MAJESTY'S SECRET SERVICE"
starring GEORGE LAZENBY · DIANA RIGG · TELLY SAVALAS as Blofeld
also starring GABRIELE FERZETTI and ILSE STEPPAT Produced by ALBERT R. BROCCOLI and HARRY SALTZMAN Directed by PETER HUNT Screenplay by RICHARD MAIBAUM
PANAVISION TECHNICOLOR

United Artists

Sea
Ja
"
Ar
PANAVISION®· TECHNICOLOR®
starring JILL ST. JOHN as 'TIFFANY CASE' CHARL
also starring LANA WOOD as 'PLENTY O'TOOLE'· JIMMY D
Produced by HARRY SALTZMAN and ALBERT R. BROCCOLI
Directed by GUY HAMILTON · Screenplay by RICHARD MAIBAUM and TOM

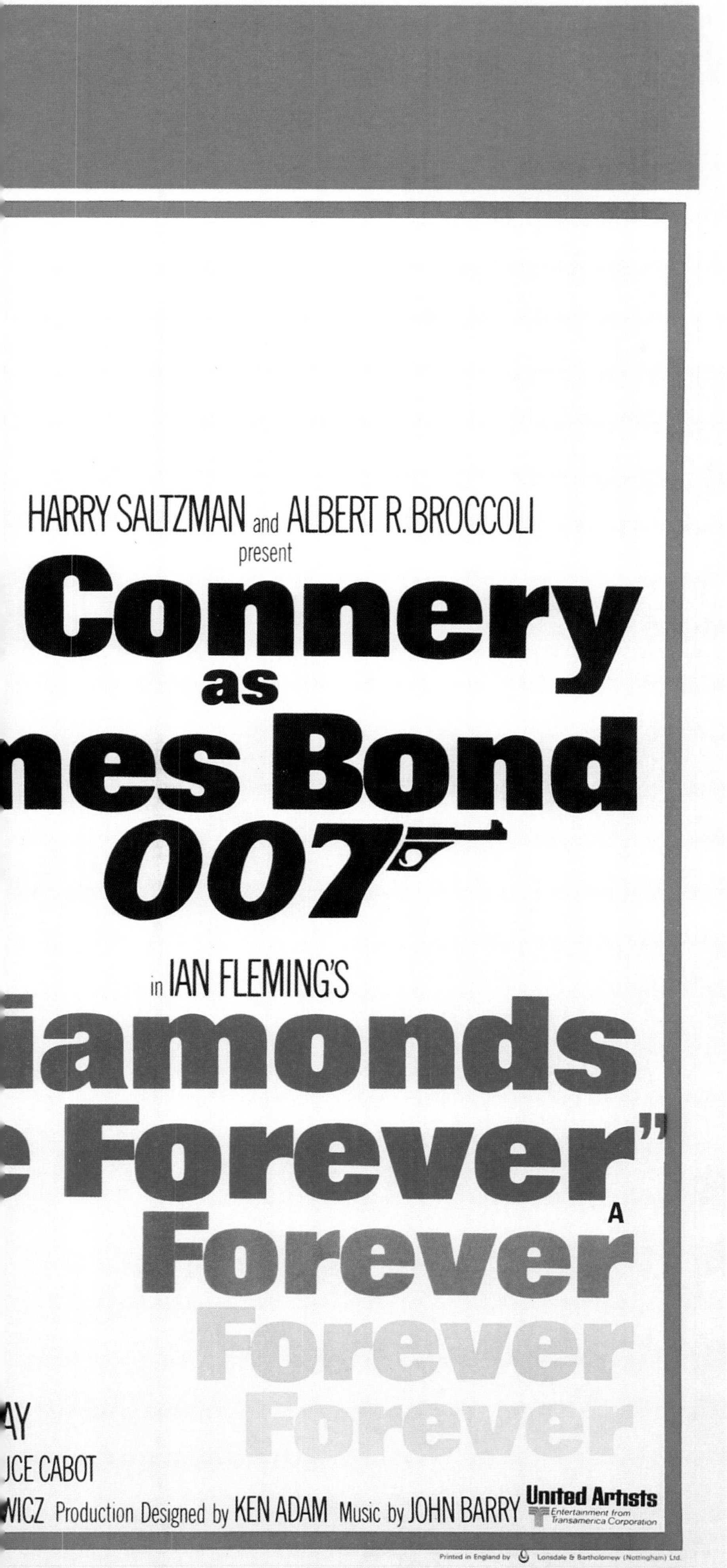

1971
Diamonds Are Forever

The comeback of the ever-popular Sean Connery was one of the greatest selling points of *Diamonds Are Forever*. The movie marked the return of the larger-than-life, charismatic Bond for which audiences yearned. There had been suggestions that the Bond phenomenon was over with the coming and going of Connery and the brief appearance of George Lazenby, labelled 'the one-hit wonder'. However, such predictions had been somewhat premature as audiences rushed to the cinema for the return of their hero. *Goldfinger* director Guy Hamilton was back too, lending the film his unique light-hearted but sophisticated touch.

James Bond is sent to Las Vegas to track down thieves who are stealing large shipments of diamonds before they reach the international market. Yet again, Bond discovers that Blofeld is the culprit. 007 is more determined than ever to catch him, as he now has the death of his late wife Tracy to avenge. Blofeld has also kidnapped billionaire Willard Whyte and has taken over his diamond-encrusted satellite, which has the power to destroy major cities. It is up to Bond to stop him.

Robert McGinnis's glamorous poster artwork was used throughout the West after a slight adjustment was made. It had been noticed that within his artwork Sean Connery appeared to be shorter than the two girls by his side, so United Artists' Head of Publicity decided to lengthen Connery's neck, to make him appear taller.

British 30 x 40 in (76 x 102 cm)
Artist/Illustrator Robert McGinnis
Date of release December 1971

Japanese 58 x 20 in (147 x 51 cm)
Date of release December 1971

Japanese 28 x 20 in (71 x 51 cm)
(Style B)

面白さとスケールをアップしてショーン・コネリーが帰って来た！
■ラスベガスの息詰る大ギャンブル——想像を絶するトリックが謎を消し、謎を生む。
■ダウンタウンで車のアクロバット追跡戦
アストンマーチンからムスタング・マッハ1へ アクロバットカーのハイ・ジャンプ
■ボンドガールも超A級——さすが大物と日本中のマスコミをさわがせた来日スターのラナ。プレイガール№1のジルが正体不明の女となって。
■ダイヤモンドの人工衛星
青い地球を空に見て、ボンド宇宙へとび出す。
ワルサーPPKにサイレンサー ぴったりきまるかっこよさ
シリーズ007弾は宇宙へとび出し007つの巨大な見せ場
これぞ、世界のダイヤをあつめた人工衛星。屈折レーザー光線がニューヨーク／モスクワを破壊する。
HARRY SALTZMAN and ALBERT R. BROCCOLI
Sean Connery as James Bond 007
IAN FLEMING'S
Diamonds Are Forever
宙をとび斜めに壁をつたわってボンドが見せるスタント・ドライブ
これが話題の月面走行車 ムーン・バギー
007
■ショーン・コネリー——ジェームズ・ボンド
テクニカラー／パナビジョン
ダイヤモンドは永遠に
ジル・セント・ジョン
チャールズ・グレイ
ジミー・ディーン
■ボンド・ガールズ
ラナ・ウッド／トリナ・パークス
ドナ・ギャラット／ルイス・マクスウェル
United Artists
ユナイト映画
映倫
原作／イアン・フレミング■製作ハリー・サルツマン／アルバート・ブロッコリ■監督ガイ・ハミルトン■音楽ジョン・バリー■主題歌シャーリー・バッシー＊サントラ盤／ユナイトレコード

Spanish 39 x 27 in (99 x 69 cm)
Artist/Illustrator Robert McGinnis
Date of release December 1971
Translation: *Diamonds For Eternity*

The scantily clad women accompanying Bond have had additional clothing added to soften the overt sexuality. The diamonds in one of the woman's hand were also raised from crotch-level in order to avoid any offence.

British 30 x 20 in (76 x 51 cm)
(Advance)
Artist/Illustrator Robert McGinnis

DIAMONDS
ARE FOREVER
A

28 x 19 in (70 x 48 cm)
(Unused artwork)

28 x 19 in (70 x 48 cm)
(Unused artwork)

ALBERT R. BROCCOLI and HARRY SALTZMAN present
Sean Connery as James Bond 007
in IAN FLEMING'S Diamonds are forever

DEVIL
DEATH
LOVERS
FORTUNE
NC3474

1973

Live And Let Die

The first important task facing the producers of the next film of the series was to choose an exciting but credible Bond, and someone who could keep the character alive. Roger Moore had a solid background in TV action dramas, with long-standing success in *The Saint* and *The Persuaders*. Rather than mimicking Sean Connery, Moore allowed his own persona to shine through and invented a new, more light-hearted Bond. Despite initial worries over the effect of having an inconsistent Bond, *Live And Let Die* was even more successful than *Diamonds Are Forever*, with box-office takings over $130 million.

Following the deaths of several other British agents, Bond becomes suspicious of the link between Harlem crime boss Mr Big and San Monique's dictator Dr Kananga in New York. After being captured, Bond meets Kananga's kept woman Solitaire, who has psychic powers. However, these powers could disappear if she loses her virginity. On his escape, Bond seduces Solitaire, who helps him discover a field containing enough poppies to guarantee its owner a monopoly over the world's heroin market.

Live And Let Die was bold for its time – an inter-racial romance involving Bond, and some of America's strongest black talent in leading roles – and yet the marketing department was worried that featuring villains played by black artistes on the poster would upset the black community. Robert McGinnis provided the artwork for the main campaign, with a detailed and stylish illustration that captured the voodoo theme of the film, along with the famous boat-chase sequence.

British 30 x 40 in (76 x 102 cm)
Artist/Illustrator Robert McGinnis
Date of release July 1973

Japanese 58 x 20 in (147 x 51 cm)
Featuring artwork by Robert McGinnis
Date of release July 1973
Translation: *The Dead Slave*

British 30 x 20 in (76 x 51 cm)
(Style A)

This poster made simple but effective use of the 007 logo, by linking it to Roger Moore's name.

British 30 x 20 in (76 x 51 cm)
(Style B)

James Bond escapes the "bad guys" with spectacular 110-foot leap.

You'll be seeing it soon—what movie people call "the most exciting boat action ever put on film"—in United Artists new James Bond thriller, "Live and Let Die."

Climax of the frantic 8-minute boat chase is an incredible 110-foot leap in an Evinrude-powered Glastron GT-150, clearing two cars and a levee road, with room to spare.

We don't recommend it, unless you happen to be Roger Moore playing James Bond and backed by an experienced technical crew. The boat bottom had to be reinforced and a hidden ramp built at the precise angle in the road embankment.

Before the actual jump—which had to be right the first time—tests were made in the open water. Jump speed of the stock Evinrude 135 was increased in stages, until the desired trajectory was achieved at a boat speed of 56 mph.

Come jump day, the word had gone out and the Louisiana levee was lined with doubting locals. The crowd buzzed with excitement, then grew silent as "Agent 007" gunned the Evinrude 135 and headed for the point of no return—then broke into a wild cheer as he sailed up and over the roadway and the parked cars, landing 110 feet down the canal from the starting point.

It demonstrates the old racing adage that there's a lot more to making a boat go than the size of the horsepower label on the engine.

first in outboards

Item No. 3575

Litho in U.S.A.

US 45 x 35 in (114 x 89 cm)
(Evinrude Promotional)
Date of release June 1973

Throughout the Bond series cross-marketing posters advertised both the movie and an important product from the film, such as an Aston Martin, Omega, Bollinger champagne and, in this particular case, an Evinrude motor and Glastron speedboat.

US 18 x 13 in (46 x 32 cm)
(Glastron Promotional)

SEE 007'S LEAP FOR LIFE IN A GLASTRON

WORLD RECORD BOAT JUMP BY JAMES BOND?

In this "leap for life" a Glastron GT-150 covers 110 feet and clears a 13-foot height above a Louisiana levee to escape Mr. Big's bad guys in "Live and Let Die". In all, 17 Glastron sportboats and Glastron/Carlson jetboats run wild in an 8-minute chase climaxed by this spectacular jump. Even the bad guys are super-smart: they go after Bond in Glastron/Carlson jets! Estimated audience: 200 million.

ROGER MOORE as JAMES BOND 007

in IAN FLEMING'S

LIVE AND LET DIE

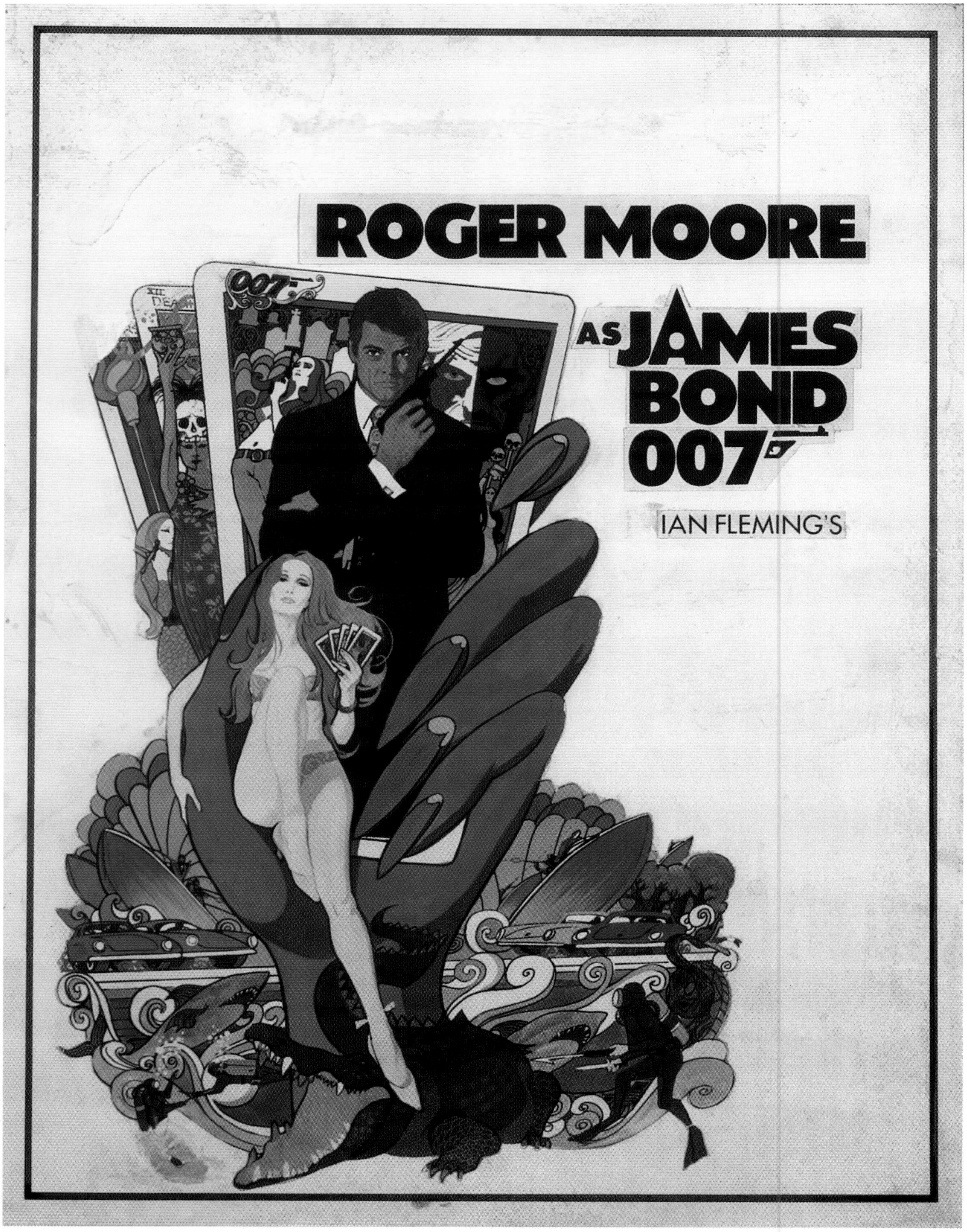

29 x 22 in (72 x 56 cm)
(Unused artwork)
Artist/Illustrator Robert McGinnis

30 x 22 in (76 x 56 cm)
(Unused poster)
Artist/Illustrator Bob Peak

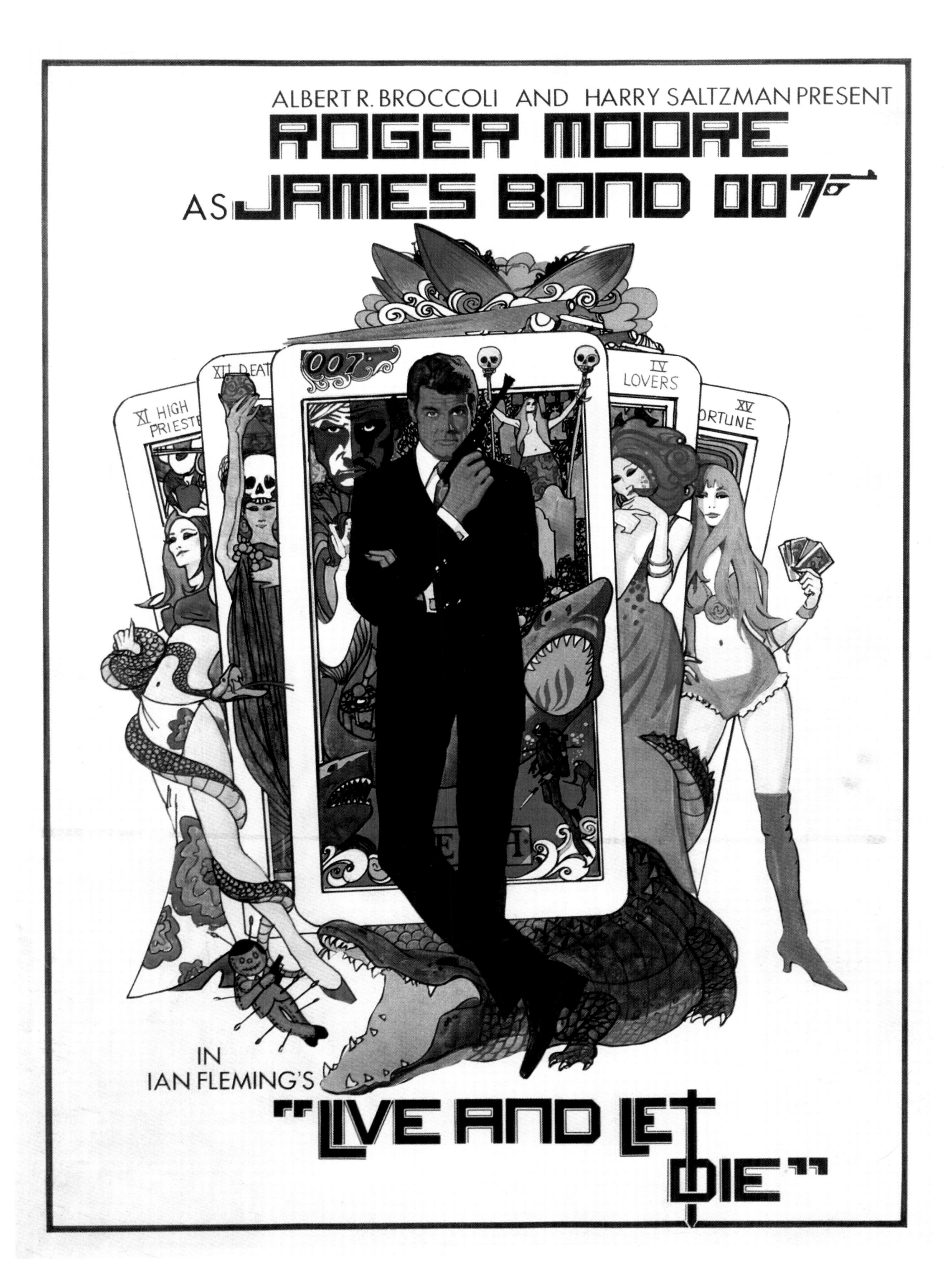
ALBERT R. BROCCOLI AND HARRY SALTZMAN PRESENT
ROGER MOORE
AS JAMES BOND 007
007
XI HIGH PRIESTE
XIII DEAT
IV LOVERS
XV ORTUNE
IN
IAN FLEMING'S
"LIVE AND LET DIE"

1974

The Man With The Golden Gun

This was the last film on which Broccoli and Saltzman worked as a team, after which it would be left up to Broccoli to maintain the high standards that they had set. Moore brought a tougher, more confident side to Bond this time around. And he faced one of the best Bond villains to date – Scaramanga, played by Christopher Lee, who was in fact a distant cousin of Ian Fleming. Nevertheless, despite these strengths the box-office grosses did not outperform *Live And Let Die*.

Bond's next mission is to recover the Solex Agitator, which has the power to convert radiation from the sun into electricity. When British Intelligence Headquarters receive a golden bullet with 007 inscribed on the side, they realize that Bond is the next target of assassin Scaramanga, who currently controls the Solex Agitator. Bond later learns of Scaramanga's evil plan to sell the device to the highest-bidding country, guaranteeing them a monopoly over the sun's energy.

Once again, McGinnis produced the main image for the worldwide campaign, which was in keeping with the traditional Bond theme. In Italy, designers contemplated producing a set of four posters showing a dismantled gun. This concept was lifted by the Americans and can be found on the US advance poster. An alternative US poster was created that, for the first time in Bond film poster history, focused on the Bond villains and is today considered a valued collectors' item.

British 30 x 40 in (76 x 102 cm)
Artist/Illustrator Robert McGinnis
Date of release December 1974

Una pistola per uccidere JAMES BOND
LA CANNA DELLA PISTOLA: UNA ROBUSTA PENNA STILOGRAFICA D'ORO
HARRY SALTZMAN e ALBERT R. BROCCOLI presentano
ROGER MOORE
nel ruolo di
JAMES BOND
AGENTE 007
L'UOMO DALLA PISTOLA D'ORO
di IAN FLEMING
DIRETTO DA GUY HAMILTON
United Artists

Una pistola per uccidere JAMES BOND
IL PERCUSSORE E L'ALLOGGIO: UN ROBUSTO ACCENDINO D'ORO
HARRY SALTZMAN e ALBERT R. BROCCOLI presentano
ROGER MOORE
nel ruolo di
JAMES BOND
AGENTE 007
L'UOMO DALLA PISTOLA D'ORO
di IAN FLEMING
DIRETTO DA GUY HAMILTON
United Artists

Una pistola per uccidere JAMES BOND
L'IMPUGNATURA: UN ROBUSTO PORTASIGARETTE D'ORO
IL GRILLETTO: UN ROBUSTO GEMELLO D'ORO
HARRY SALTZMAN e ALBERT R. BROCCOLI presentano
ROGER MOORE
nel ruolo di
JAMES BOND
AGENTE 007
L'UOMO DALLA PISTOLA D'ORO
di IAN FLEMING
DIRETTO DA GUY HAMILTON
United Artists

Una pistola per uccidere JAMES BOND
UNA ROBUSTA PENNA STILOGRAFICA D'ORO CHE SI INSERISCE NEL CORPO DI UN ACCENDINO D'ORO. UN PORTASIGARETTE D'ORO CHE SI TRASFORMA IN IMPUGNATURA. UN ROBUSTO GEMELLO D'ORO CHE DIVENTA GRILLETTO. UN SINGOLO PROIETTILE D'ORO SI INSERISCE NELLA CANNA.
L'UOMO DALLA PISTOLA D'ORO E' PRONTO AD UCCIDERE JAMES BOND
HARRY SALTZMAN e ALBERT R. BROCCOLI presentano
ROGER MOORE
nel ruolo di
JAMES BOND
AGENTE 007
L'UOMO DALLA PISTOLA D'ORO
di IAN FLEMING
DIRETTO DA GUY HAMILTON
United Artists

Italian set of 4 each 39 x 27 in (99 x 69 cm)
(Advance)
Date of release December 1974
Translation: *Agent 007 The Man With The Golden Gun*

US 41 x 27 in (104 x 69 cm)
(Advance)
Date of release December 1974

British 37 x 25 in (94 x 64 cm)
(Thai Airways)

US 41 x 27 in (104 x 69 cm)
(Advance Style B)
Artist/Illustrator Robert McGinnis

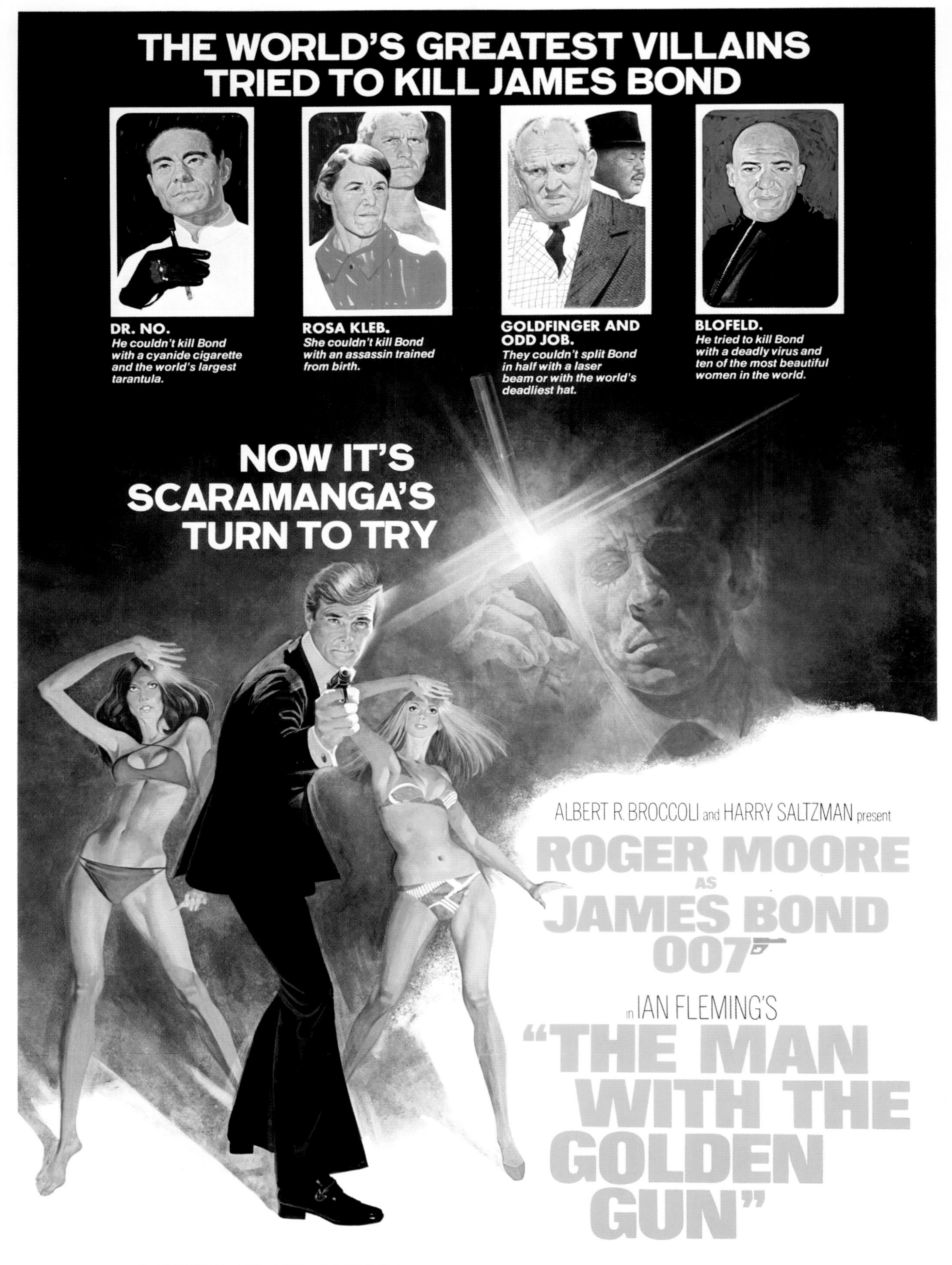

with CHRISTOPHER LEE · BRITT EKLAND · Produced by ALBERT R. BROCCOLI and HARRY SALTZMAN
Directed by GUY HAMILTON · Screenplay by RICHARD MAIBAUM and TOM MANKIEWICZ · Music by JOHN BARRY

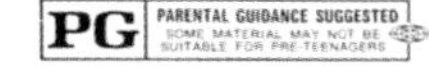

ORIGINAL MOTION PICTURE SOUNDTRACK AVAILABLE ON UNITED ARTISTS RECORDS AND TAPES

·COLOR·

United Artists
Entertainment from Transamerica Corporation

STYLE B

74/251

"THE MAN WITH THE GOLDEN GUN"

British 30 x 20 in (76 x 51 cm)
(Premium Bond)

British 30 x 20 in (76 x 51 cm)
(Du Pont)

"THE MAN WITH THE GOLDEN GUN"&
DU PONT
the Star Performers
An Eon Production released through United Artists.

ALBERT R. BROCCOLI
presents
ROGER
MOORE
as
IAN FLEMING'S
JAMES
BOND
007 in
"THE SPY WHO LO

starring BARBARA BACH
and CURT JURGENS as "Stromberg"

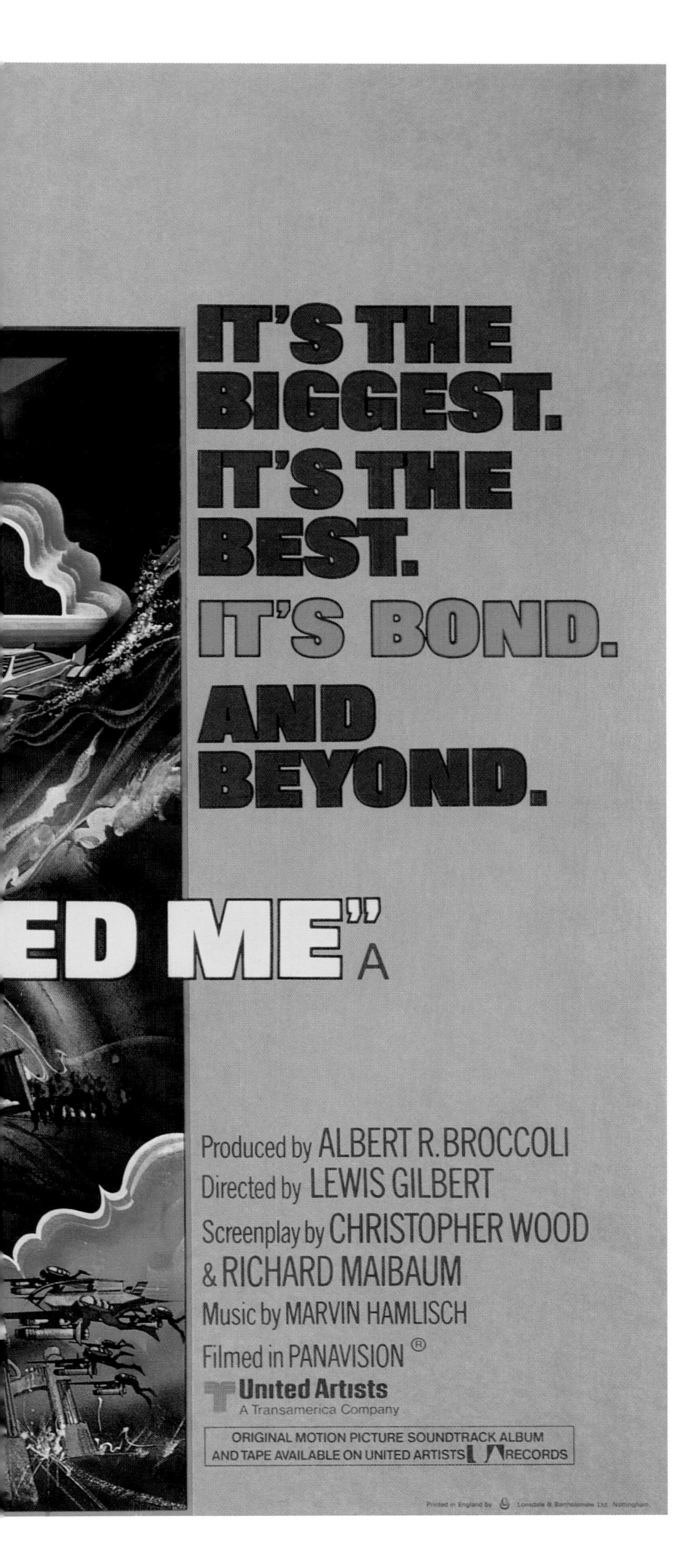

1977

The Spy Who Loved Me

Broccoli wanted *Spy* to be the biggest Bond yet and brought back director Lewis Gilbert (*You Only Live Twice*). United Artists invested a huge budget of $13.5 million to guarantee its success. The results were impressive, including the construction of the world's largest soundstage at Pinewood Studios to accommodate three full-size submarines. The exotic locations of Egypt, Sardinia and the Bahamas, combined with the highly memorable and larger-than-life villains, such as Jaws, delighted audiences and broke box-office records yet again.

Bond is assigned to accompany his Soviet spy counterpart, Major Anya Amasova, in an investigation into the loss of a number of Soviet and British submarines. Both parties believe that shipping magnate Karl Stromberg is to blame for their disappearance and they subsequently discover that he has hijacked the submarines and their crews. Stromberg plans to use the submarines as a base to launch missiles to destroy civilization on Earth, while escaping and ruling his dream underwater world.

This was the first film campaign to use Bob Peak's artwork and it was so effective that it was utilized internationally. The detailed image, cast in an Art-Nouveau style, was one of the first to depict 007 in a futuristic setting. However, due to the effects of the printing process, the faces of Moore and Barbara Bach became noticeably darker and thus less distinguishable on the poster. Peak therefore repainted these images, and so on the European posters, most notably in the Italian version, the complete illustration is clearer and both artistes are more recognizable.

British 30 x 40 in (76 x 102 cm)
Date of release July 1977

German 47 x 22 in (119 x 56 cm)
(Special display)
Date of release August 1977

È IL PIÙ SPETTACOLARE. È IL PIÙ BELLO.
VA AL DI SOPRA DI OGNI VOSTRA ASPETTATIVA!

ALBERT R. BROCCOLI presenta
ROGER MOORE
è
JAMES BOND
AGENTE 007 di IAN FLEMING
IN
"LA SPIA CHE MI AMAVA"
"THE SPY WHO LOVED ME"
con BARBARA BACH e CURT JURGENS nella parte di Stromberg · Prodotto da ALBERT R. BROCCOLI · Diretto da LEWIS GILBERT
Sceneggiatura di CHRISTOPHER WOOD e RICHARD MAIBAUM · Musica di MARVIN HAMLISCH · PANAVISION · United Artists
LA COLONNA SONORA ORIGINALE É INCISA SU DISCHI U.A. DISTR.: RICORDI
ANNO DI EDIZIONE 1977
ROTOPRESS - ROMA

Italian 28 x 13 in (71 x 33 cm)
Artist/Illustrator Bob Peak
Date of release September 1977

It's the BIGGEST.
It's the BEST. It's BOND.
And B-E-Y-O-N-D.

starring BARBARA BACH and CURT JURGENS as "Stromberg" · Produced by ALBERT R. BROCCOLI ·
Directed by LEWIS GILBERT Screenplay by CHRISTOPHER WOOD & RICHARD MAIBAUM ·
Music by MARVIN HAMLISCH · Filmed in PANAVISION® COLOR
MOTION PICTURE MUSIC ALBUM AND TAPES AVAILABLE ON UNITED ARTISTS UA RECORDS
United Artists
Distributed by
United International Pictures

Robert Burton Printers Pty. Ltd.

Australian 30 x 12 in (76 x 30 cm)
Date of release December 1977

British 30 x 20 in (76 x 51 cm)
(Advance Style A)
Artist/Illustrator Bob Peak

IT'S THE BIGGEST.
IT'S THE BEST.
IT'S BOND.
AND BEYOND.

Japanese 28 x 20 in (71 x 51 cm)
(Style B)
Date of release December 1977

Hungarian 33 x 23 in (84 x 58 cm)
Date of release May 1989

This was the original date of release for this film in Hungary and marks the first Bond film to be screened in Eastern Europe.

A KÉM, AKI
SZERETETT

BERTA GÁBOR '89

ENGEM

JAMES BOND 007

SZÍNES ANGOL KÉMFILM

FŐSZEREPBEN: ROGER MOORE,
BARBARA BACH, CURT JURGENS
RENDEZTE: LEWIS GILBERT

F. k.: Stenczer Noémi PRIMO – OFFSET

FOR
SUMMER
007
"THE
SPY WHO
LOVED ME"
United Artists

IT'S THE BIGGEST.
"THE
SPY WHO
LOVED
ME"
FOR
AUTUMN 007
FROM
United Artists
Biggest stage ever built for a motion picture — the supertanker interior which nests 3 nuclear submarines.

IT'S THE BEST.
"THE
SPY WHO
LOVED
ME"
FOR
AUTUMN 007
FROM
United Artists

IT'S BOND. AND BEYOND.
"THE
SPY WHO
LOVED ME"
FOR
SUMMER 007
FROM
United Artists

US set of 4 each 20 x 60 in (51 x 152 cm)
Date of release July 1977

British 81 x 30 in (205 x 77 cm)

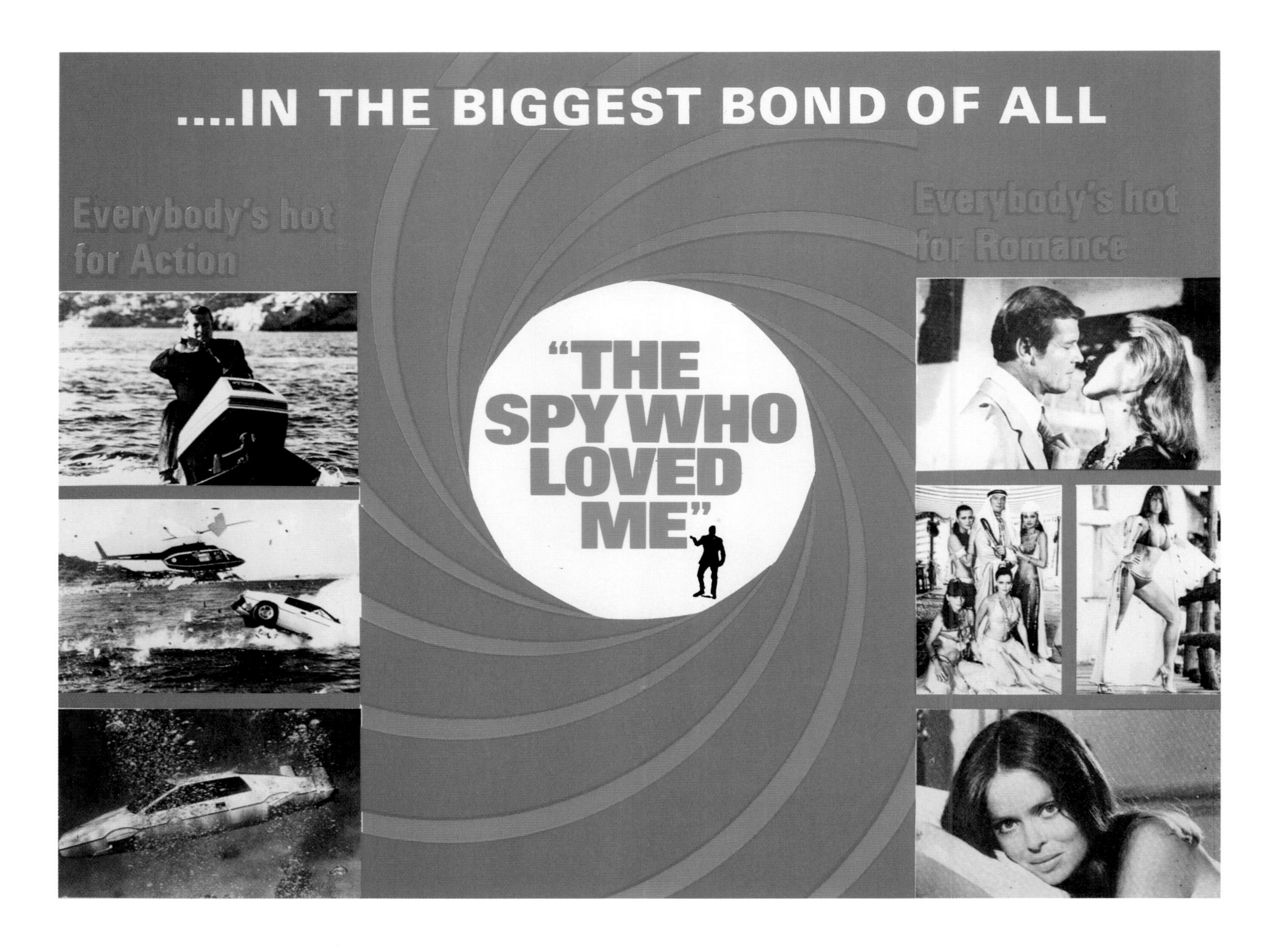

British 30 x 40 in (76 x 102 cm)
(Marler Haley)

These posters were designed by the company Marler Haley, solely for use in Odeon cinemas.

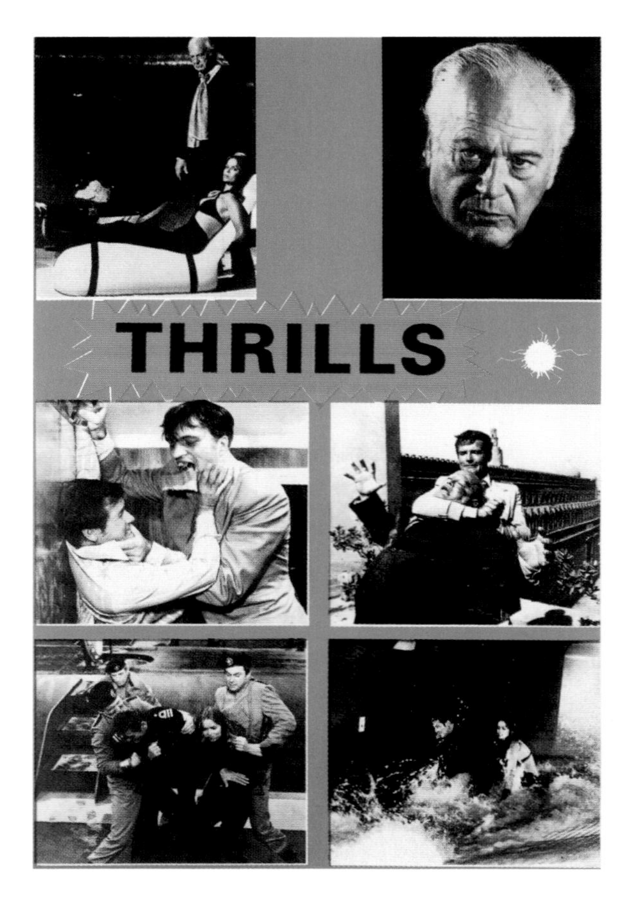

British set of 4 each 30 x 20 in (76 x 51 cm)
(Marler Haley)

007 BLASTS BACK

ROGER MOORE
AS JAMES BOND

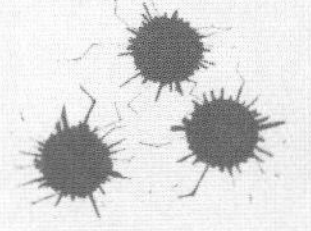

BARBARA BACH
AS THE BEAUTIFUL SPY ANYA

the
J. BOND
007
Starring
Richard Kiel as 'Jaws' and
Directed by Lewis
Music by John Barr
Executive Producer
ORIGINAL MOTION PICTURE SOUNDTRACK
ON UNITED ARTISTS RECORDS AND TAPES.
Filmed in PANAVISION® DOLBY STEREO

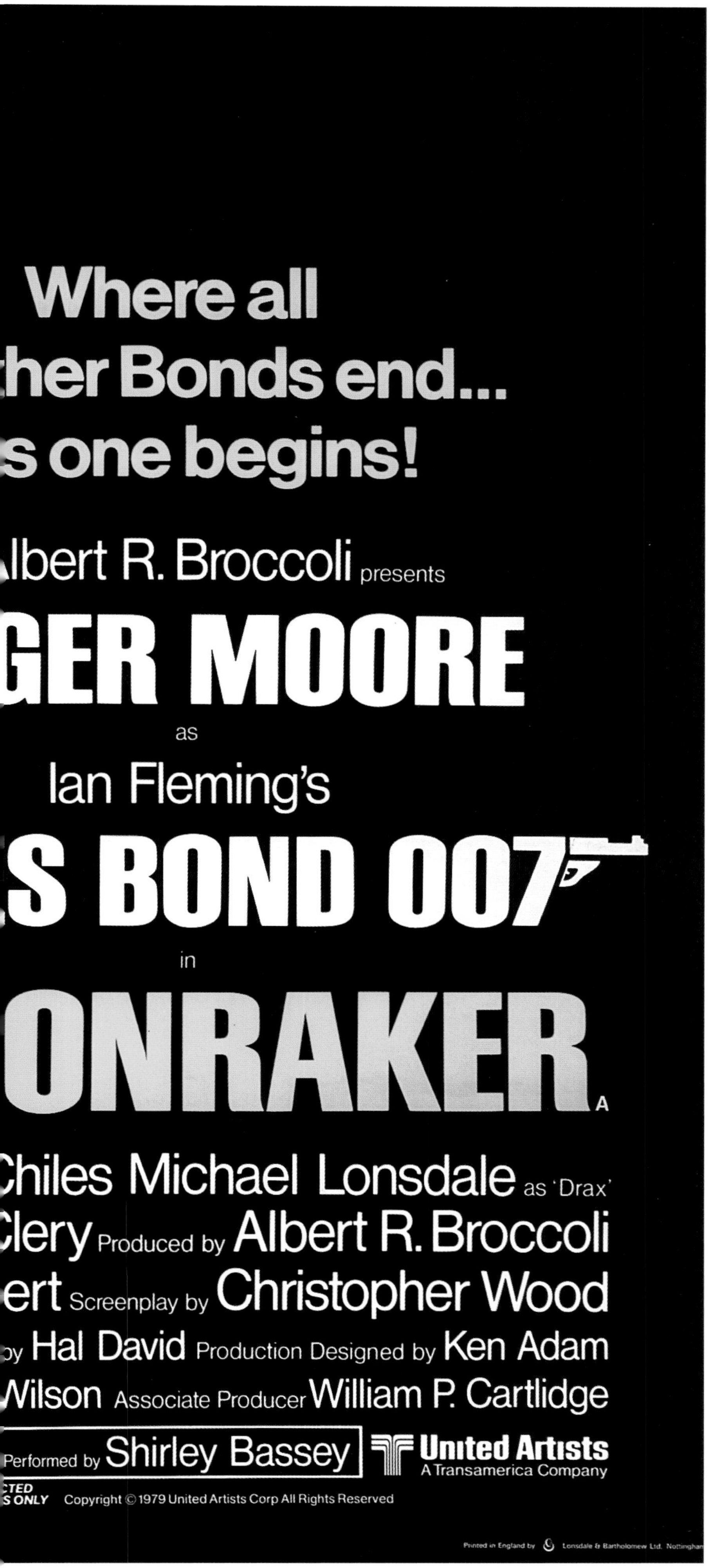

1979

Moonraker

Blofeld may have interrupted Bond's expedition to the stars in *You Only Live Twice* but this time the producers finally sent Bond into outer space. Concerned that Fleming's novel had become somewhat dated by the late 1970s, the producers added screenwriter Christopher Wood to the creative team, hoping to modernize the story while retaining the essence of the characters. The film was nominated for an Oscar in special effects and broke all previous Bond box-office records.

Bond is sent to California to interrogate Hugo Drax, whom he believes is responsible for the disappearance of the American space shuttle Moonraker. Living up to his reputation, Bond seduces Drax's employee Corinne Dufour, who confirms his suspicions. 007 then meets Holly Goodhead, who is also trying to investigate Drax. At Drax's laboratory in the Brazilian jungle, the two discover that he is producing a deadly gas, with the power to destroy the Earth – after which he plans to live as the leader of a master race in his kingdom in space.

Dan Gouzee designed a number of illustrations for *Moonraker*. Each design focused on a different classic Bondian element, such as the action, the Bond girls and, for this film in particular, the futuristic set. These complete images were used throughout the British and American campaigns, and many of the European posters also featured his artwork.

British 30 x 40 in (76 x 102 cm)
Artist/Illustrator Dan Gouzee
Date of release June 1979

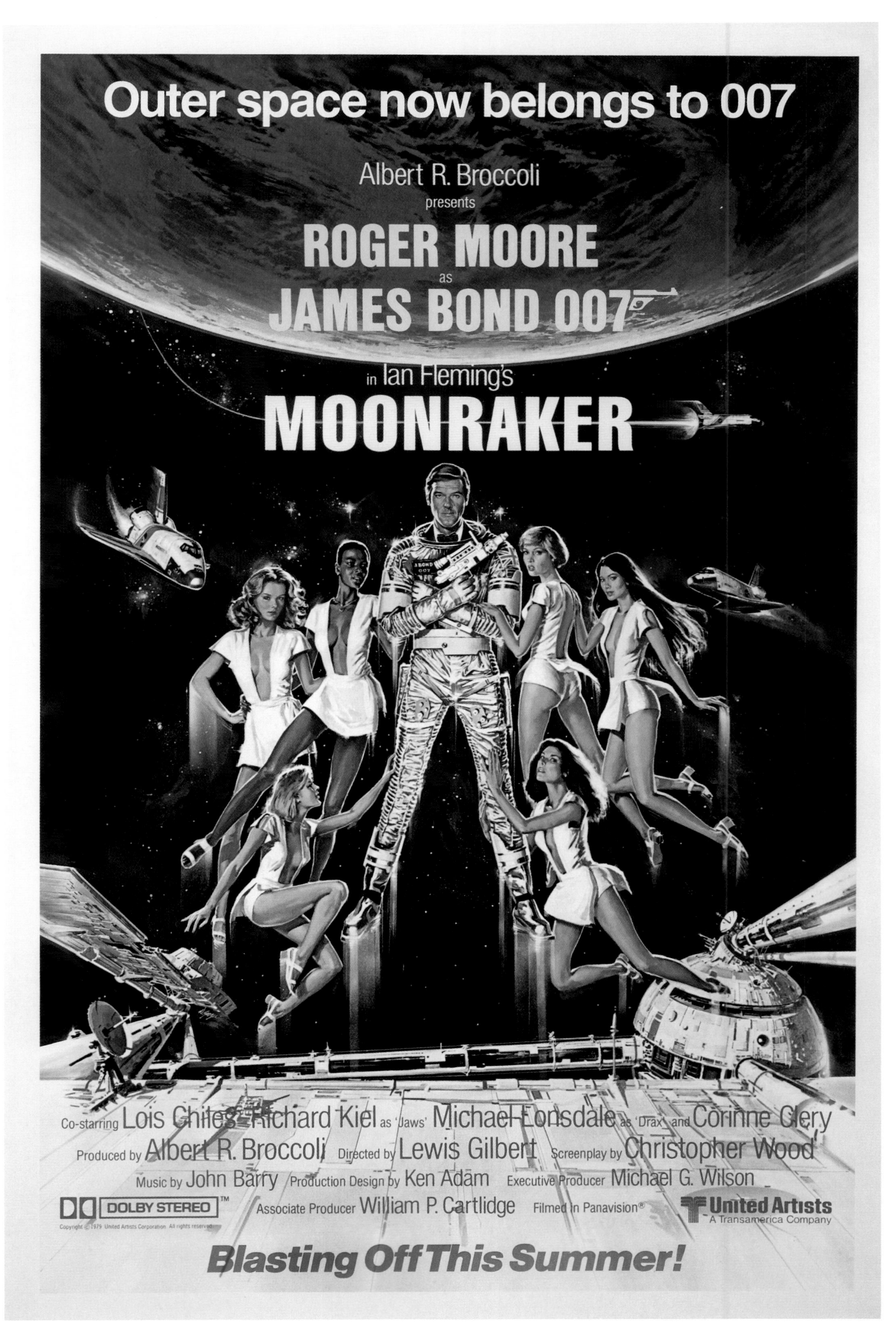

US 41 x 27 in (104 x 69 cm)
(Advance Style B)
Artist/Illustrator Dan Gouzee
Date of release June 1979

US 41 x 27 in (104 x 69 cm)
(International Style B)
Artist/Illustrator Dan Gouzee

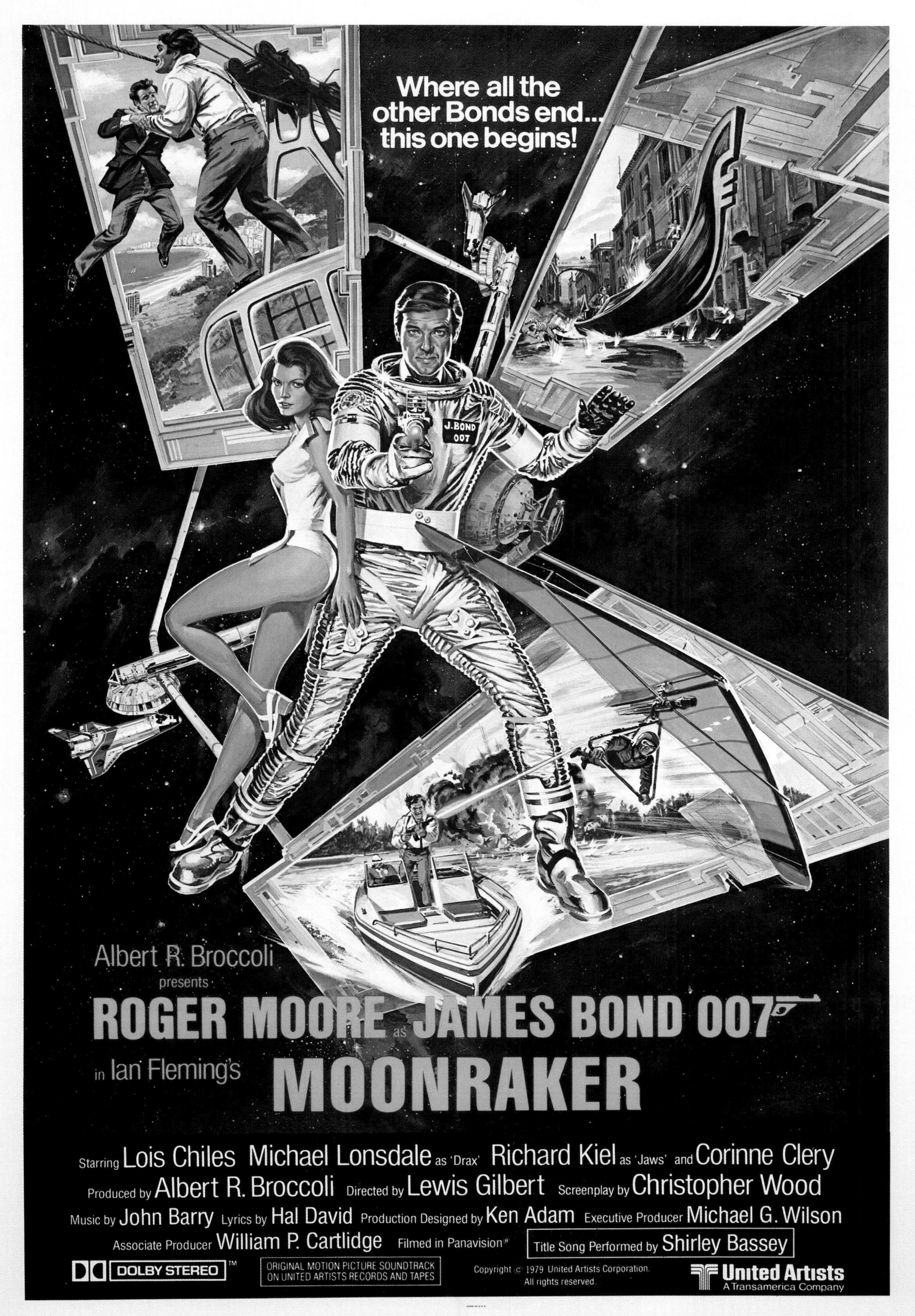
Where all the
other Bonds end...
this one begins!
J. BOND
007
Albert R. Broccoli
presents
ROGER MOORE as JAMES BOND 007
in Ian Fleming's
MOONRAKER
Starring Lois Chiles Michael Lonsdale as 'Drax' Richard Kiel as 'Jaws' and Corinne Clery
Produced by Albert R. Broccoli Directed by Lewis Gilbert Screenplay by Christopher Wood
Music by John Barry Lyrics by Hal David Production Designed by Ken Adam Executive Producer Michael G. Wilson
Associate Producer William P. Cartlidge Filmed in Panavision®
Title Song Performed by Shirley Bassey
DOLBY STEREO™
ORIGINAL MOTION PICTURE SOUNDTRACK
ON UNITED ARTISTS RECORDS AND TAPES
Copyright © 1979 United Artists Corporation.
All rights reserved.
United Artists
A Transamerica Company
1 SHT. STYLE B. INT'L MOONRAKER

US 41 x 27 in (104 x 69 cm)
(Right Advance, One Stop)
Featuring artwork by Robert McGinnis

In the late 1970s, United Artists introduced a new style of poster campaign. These were called 'One Stops' and always contained two differently styled one sheets and a set of lobby cards. These were printed on one sheet of paper and enabled the cinema owner to choose which posters he wished to display, in a more economical way. This new style proved unpopular and so they were used only in 1979 before the idea was abandoned.

MOONRAKER
JAMES BOND 007
MOONRAKER
United Artists
A Transamerica Company

US 41 x 27 in (104 x 69 cm)
(Left Advance, One Stop)
Featuring artwork by Robert McGinnis

US 41 x 27 in (104 x 69 cm)
(Advance Style A)
Artist/Illustrator Dan Gouzee

Outer space now belongs to 007.

Albert R. Broccoli
presents
ROGER MOORE
is
JAMES BOND 007
in Ian Fleming's
MOONRAKER

J.BOND 007

Co-Starring Lois Chiles Richard Kiel as 'Jaws' Michael Lonsdale as 'Drax'
Produced by Albert R. Broccoli Directed by Lewis Gilbert Screenplay by Christopher Wood
Music by John Barry Production Design by Ken Adam

Blasting Off Next Summer.

United Artists
A Transamerica Company

MOONRAKER ADVANCE 1 SHEET "A"

Printed in U.S.A.

US set of 4 each 20 x 60 in (51 x 152 cm)
Featuring artwork by Dan Gouzee

German 33 x 23 in (84 x 58 cm)
Featuring artwork by Dan Gouzee
Date of release March 1979
Translation: *Moonraker – Top Secret*

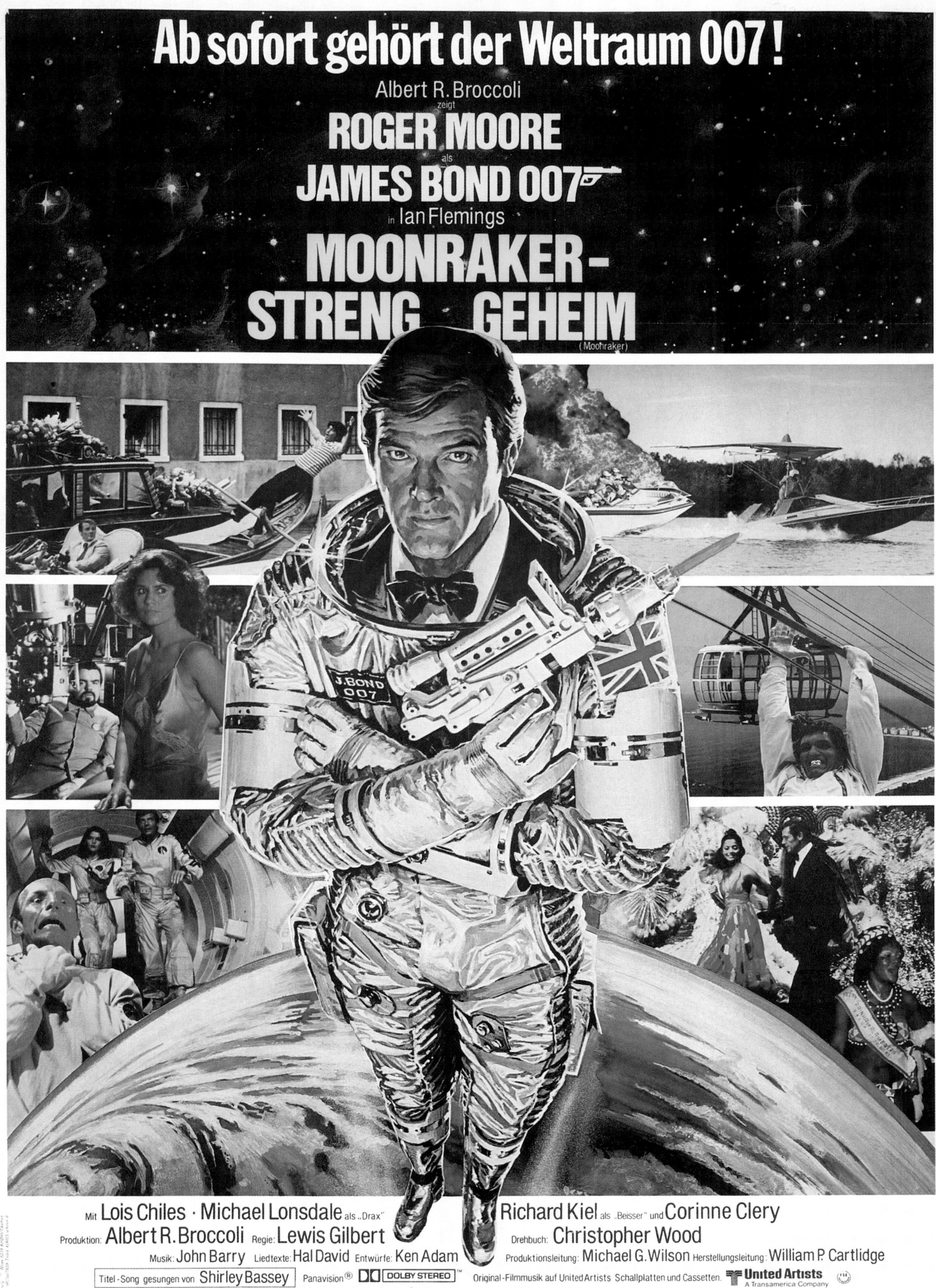
Ab sofort gehört der Weltraum 007!
Albert R. Broccoli
zeigt
ROGER MOORE
als
JAMES BOND 007
in Ian Flemings
MOONRAKER -
STRENG GEHEIM
(Moonraker)
J. BOND
007
Mit Lois Chiles · Michael Lonsdale als „Drax" Richard Kiel als „Beisser" und Corinne Clery
Produktion: Albert R. Broccoli Regie: Lewis Gilbert Drehbuch: Christopher Wood
Musik: John Barry Liedtexte: Hal David Entwürfe: Ken Adam Produktionsleitung: Michael G. Wilson Herstellungsleitung: William P. Cartlidge
Titel-Song gesungen von Shirley Bassey
Panavision®
DOLBY STEREO
Original-Filmmusik auf United Artists Schallplatten und Cassetten.
United Artists
A Transamerica Company
Copyright © 1979 United Artists Corporation. All rights reserved

ALBERT R. BROCCOLI presents
ROGER MOORE as IAN FLEMING'S JAMES B
IN FOR YOUR EYES O
STARRING CAROLE BOUQUET · TOPOL · LYNN-HOLLY JOHNSON · JULIAN
PRODUCED BY ALBERT R. BROCCOLI · DIRECTED BY JOHN GLEN · SCREENPLAY BY RICHARD MAIBAUM AND MICHAEL
MUSIC BY BILL CONTI · PRODUCTION DESIGNER PETER LAMONT · ASSOCIATE PRODUCER TOM PEVSNER PANAVISION® TECHNICOLOR® DOLBY STEREO™ IN SELECTED THEATRES

1981

For Your Eyes Only

Broccoli approached this film with a new emphasis on realism, which was initially greeted with scepticism by many fans. Executive producer Michael Wilson joined Dick Maibaum on the writing team and together they wrote the following five Bond screenplays. In addition, *For Your Eyes Only* marked the directorial debut of a long-time Bond editor, John Glen. He asked Moore to portray the role more seriously, with the effect that the jokes were downplayed and Bond began to rely on his instincts as a spy again, rather than high-tech gadgets.

St Georges, a British spy ship, has accidentally sunk in Albanian territorial waters. On board is the ATAC, a top-secret communications device that is used by the British to send launch instructions to their Polaris submarines. Bond has to recover the ATAC, but once the Russians realize the potential of the device to cause havoc, a race commences between the two nations to gain control of it.

Hy Smith, Head of Publicity for United Artists, hired Bill Gold to design a completely original and fresh campaign. Gold created a highly controversial design that has come to be known as the 'Legs Campaign'. It was felt that outside the US, the audiences would need more visual action on which to focus, and so the artwork featured extra details around the legs.

British 30 x 40 in (76 x 102 cm)
Designer Bill Gold
Date of release June 1981

Japanese 28 x 20 in (71 x 51 cm)
(Advance Style B)
Date of release July 1981
Translation: *Your Eyes Only*

Japanese 28 x 20 in (71 x 51 cm)
(Style B)
Artist/Illustrator Hisamitsu Noguchi

―危機また危機へ！
シリーズ中、最も多くの
007アクションを
投入した――
スーパー巨篇!!
◆空中のヘリコプター戦！
陸の凄絶カーチェイス！海の水中戦！
さらに白銀の世界へ飛んで、
ボンドが見せる最高のスキーアクション！
クライマックスは登はん不可能の絶壁へ
決死の挑戦――!!
TURBO ESPRIT
FOR YOUR 007 EYES ONLY
007
最新作・第12弾！
ユア・アイズ・オンリー
ロジャー・ムーア=007
キャロル・ブーケ◆トポル◆リン・ホリー・ジョンソン
ジュリアン・グロバー◆カサンドラ・ハリス
DOLBY STEREO
ALBERT R. BROCCOLI presents
ROGER MOORE
as IAN FLEMING'S
JAMES BOND 007
in
FOR YOUR EYES ONLY
Starring CAROLE BOUQUET · TOPOL · LYNN-HOLLY JOHNSON · JULIAN GLOVER
Produced by ALBERT R. BROCCOLI · Directed by JOHN GLEN
Screenplay by RICHARD MAIBAUM and MICHAEL G. WILSON
Executive Producer MICHAEL G. WILSON
Title Song Performed by SHEENA EASTON
製作アルバート・ブロッコリ◆監督ジョン・グレン
脚本リチャード・メイバウム◆音楽ビル・コンティ(サントラ盤・ユナイトレコード)
主題曲シーナ・イーストン(東芝EMI)◆カラー作品
United Artists
ユナイト映画
映倫

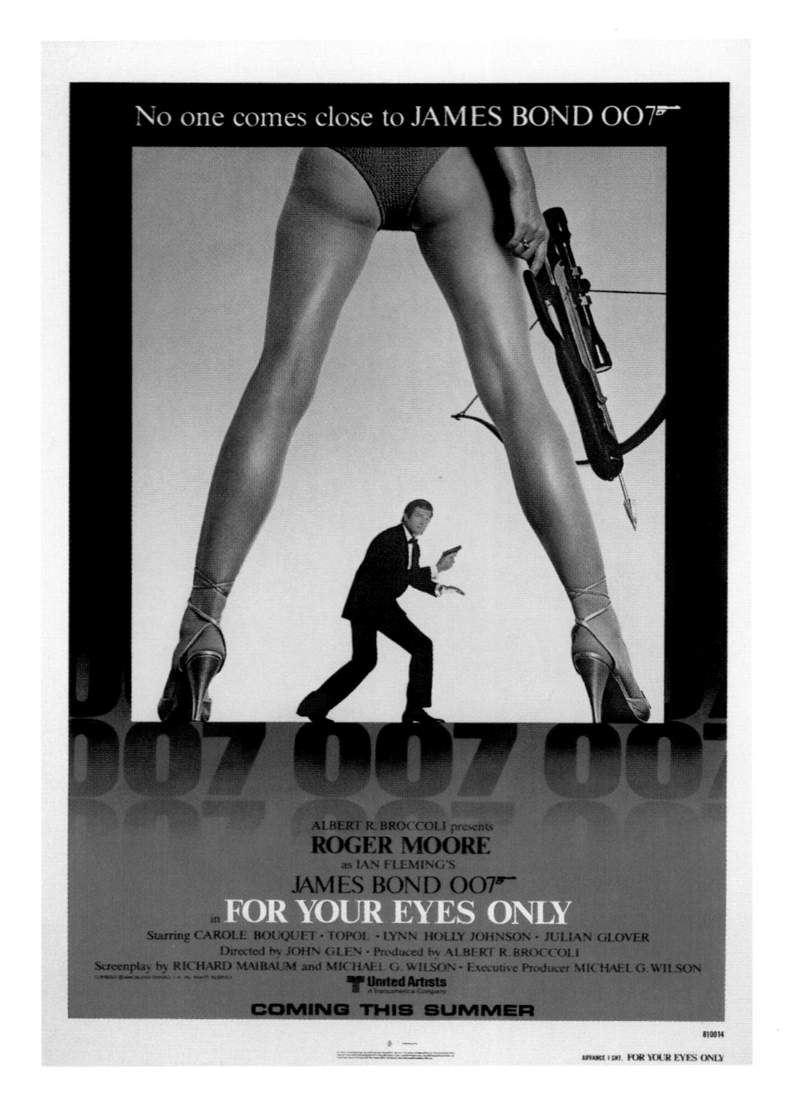

US 41 x 27 in (104 x 69 cm)
(Advance)
Designer Bill Gold
Date of release June 1981

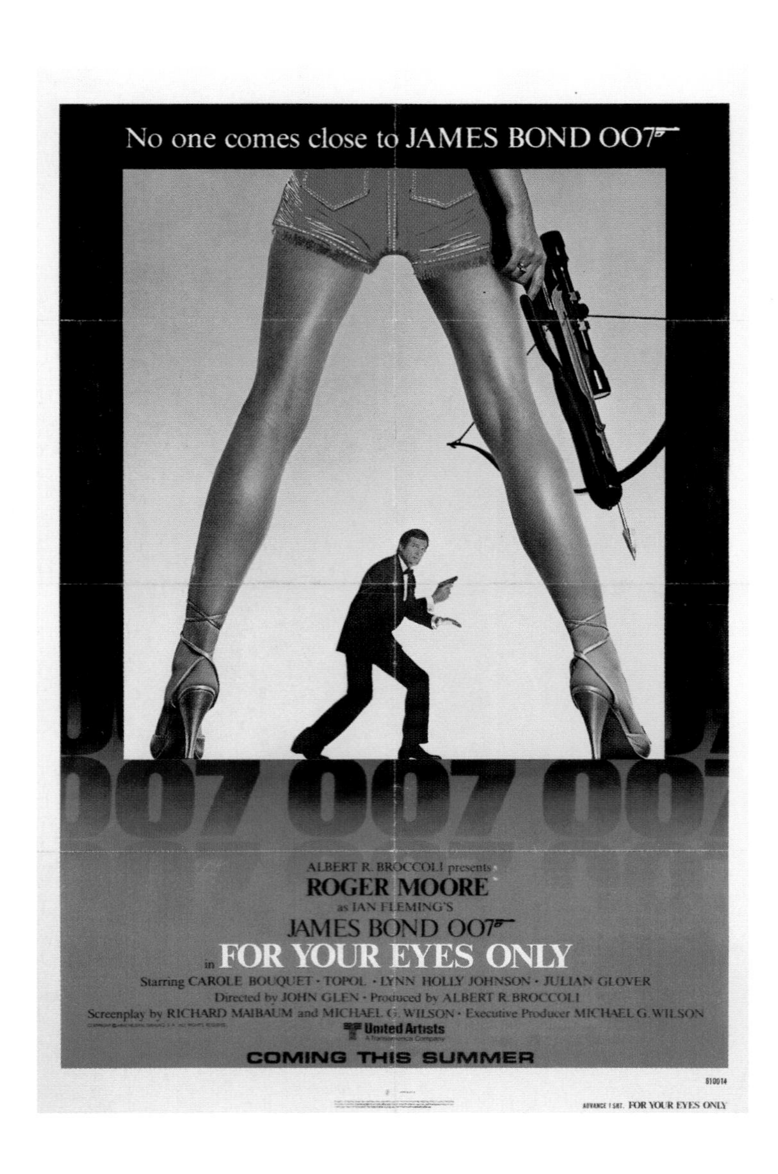

US 41 x 27 in (104 x 69 cm)
(Advance)
Designer Bill Gold

The above image caused controversy in a number of more conservative American states, including Philadelphia and Utah, because of the amount of uncovered flesh that was visible. As a result, cinema owners superimposed a larger pair of shorts to ensure that people would not be offended.

Japanese 28 x 20 in (71 x 51 cm)
(Style A)

ALBERT R. BROCCOLI presents
ROGER MOORE
as IAN FLEMING'S
JAMES BOND 007
in
FOR YOUR EYES ONLY
Starring CAROLE BOUQUET · TOPOL · LYNN-HOLLY JOHNSON · JULIAN GLOVER
Produced by ALBERT R. BROCCOLI · Directed by JOHN GLEN
Screenplay by RICHARD MAIBAUM AND MICHAEL G. WILSON
Executive Producer MICHAEL G. WILSON
最新作・第12弾！
—危機また危機へ！
シリーズ最大のスケールで
007アクションを叩き込んだ
スーパー巨篇——!!
FOR YOUR 007 EYES ONLY
007 ユア・アイズ・オンリー
ロジャー・ムーア＝007
◆キャロル・ブーケ◆トポル◆リン＝ホリー・ジョンソン◆ジュリアン・グロバー◆カサンドラ・ハリス
◆製作アルバート・ブロッコリ◆監督ジョン・グレン◆脚本リチャード・メイバウム
◆音楽ビル・コンティ（サントラ盤/ユナイトレコード）◆主題歌シーナ・イーストン（東芝EMI）◆カラー作品
United Artists
A Transamerica Company
ユナイト映画
DOLBY STEREO
IN SELECTED THEATRES
映倫
56008

British 30 x 40 in (76 x 102 cm)
(Marler Haley)

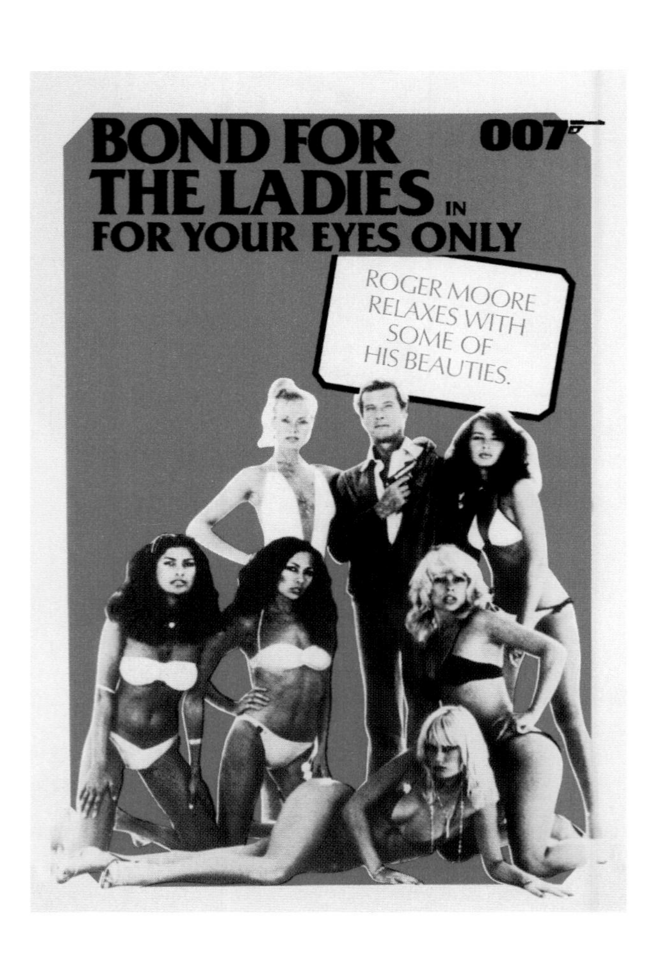

BOND FOR THE LADIES IN
007
FOR YOUR EYES ONLY
ROGER MOORE RELAXES WITH SOME OF HIS BEAUTIES.

British set of 4 each
30 x 20 in (76 x 51 cm)
(Marler Haley)

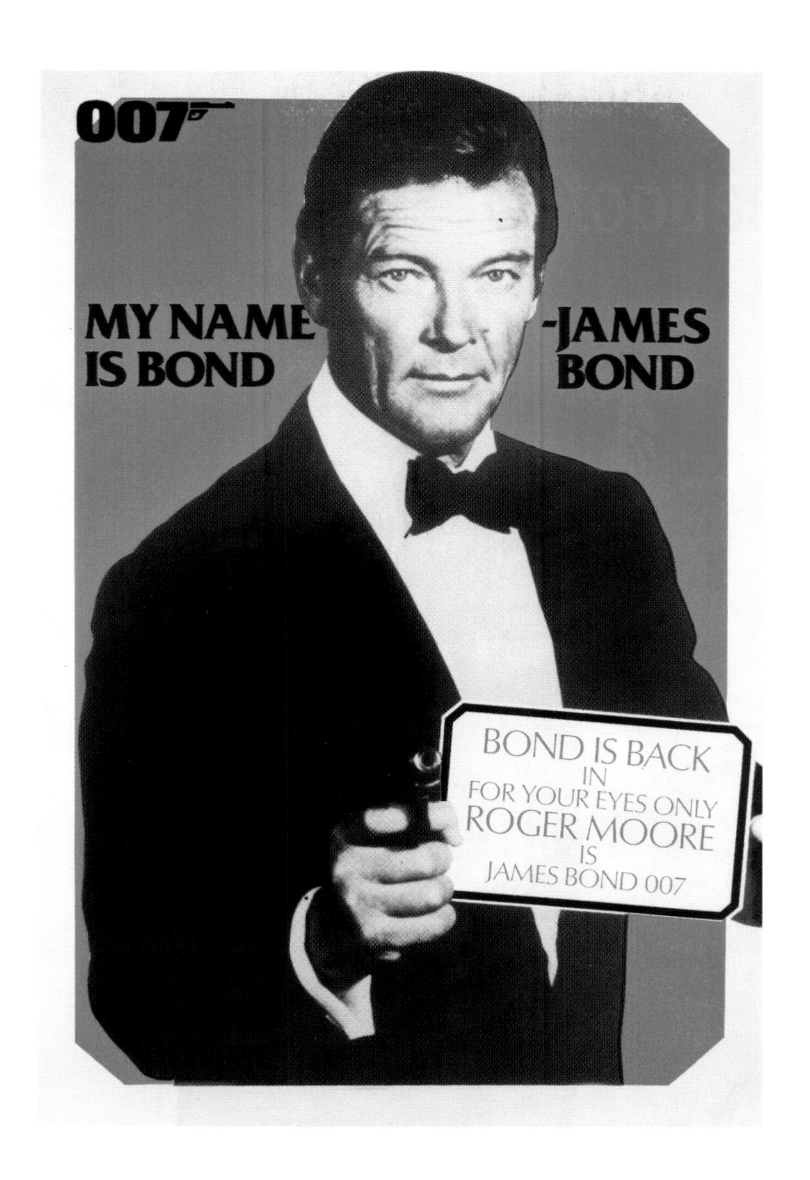
007
MY NAME IS BOND
-JAMES BOND
BOND IS BACK
IN
FOR YOUR EYES ONLY
ROGER MOORE
IS
JAMES BOND 007

007
BOND FOR ACTION
IN
FOR YOUR EYES ONLY
ROGER MOORE
JAMES BOND 007
FIGHTS HIS WAY
OUT OF A
TIGHT CORNER.

Japanese 28 x 20 in (71 x 51 cm)
(Yamakatsu poster)
Date of release July 1983

Japanese 28 x 20 in (71 x 51 cm)
(Advance)

This design was taken from elements of Maurice Binder's title sequence.

◆アルバート・R・ブロッコリ製作◆
ロジャー・ムーア=ジェームズ・ボンド007
OCTOPUSSY
007オクトパシー
最新第13弾 '83・夏・公開!
United Artists

US 41 x 27 in (104 x 69 cm)
Artist/Illustrator Renato Casaro

Thai 31 x 21 in (79 x 54 cm)
Featuring artwork by Renato Casaro
Date of release February 1984

ไซโก SEIKO
เทคโนโลยีแห่งเวลาที่ล้ำหน้า ภูมิใจเสนอ
ยิ่งยอดของอาวุธ พิเศษสุดด้วยฝีมือ
เขาคือเจมส์ บอนด์ 007 กลเม็ดเหนือชั้น
บู๊สะบั้นหั่นแหลก แหวกแนว ทั้งบนบก
ในน้ำ และกลางอากาศ
โรเจอร์ มัวร์
ตัวเก่ง เป็น
007
เพชฌฆาต
ปลาหมึกยักษ์
ม๊อด อดัมส์
หลุยส์ จูร์ดัง
คาบีร์ เบดี
คริสตีน่า เวย์บอร์น
จอห์น เกลน
กำกับการแสดง
ROGER MOORE
JAMES BOND 007
OCTOPUSSY
MAUD ADAMS, LOUIS JOURDAN, KRISTINA WAYBORN, KABIR BEDI, VIJAY AMRITRAJ
Produced by ALBERT R. BROCCOLI Directed by JOHN GLEN Screenstory and Screenplay by GEORGE MacDONALD FRASER and RICHARD MAIBAUM & MICHAEL G. WILSON
Executive Producer MICHAEL G. WILSON Production Designer PETER LAMONT Associate Producer TOM PEVSNER
Music by JOHN BARRY SOUNDTRACK AVAILABLE ON RECORDS AND TAPES RITA COOLIDGE
ไซโก นาฬิกาที่เจมส์ บอนด์สวมใส่
ใน "007 เพชฌฆาตปลาหมึกยักษ์"
ฉายที่
วันที่

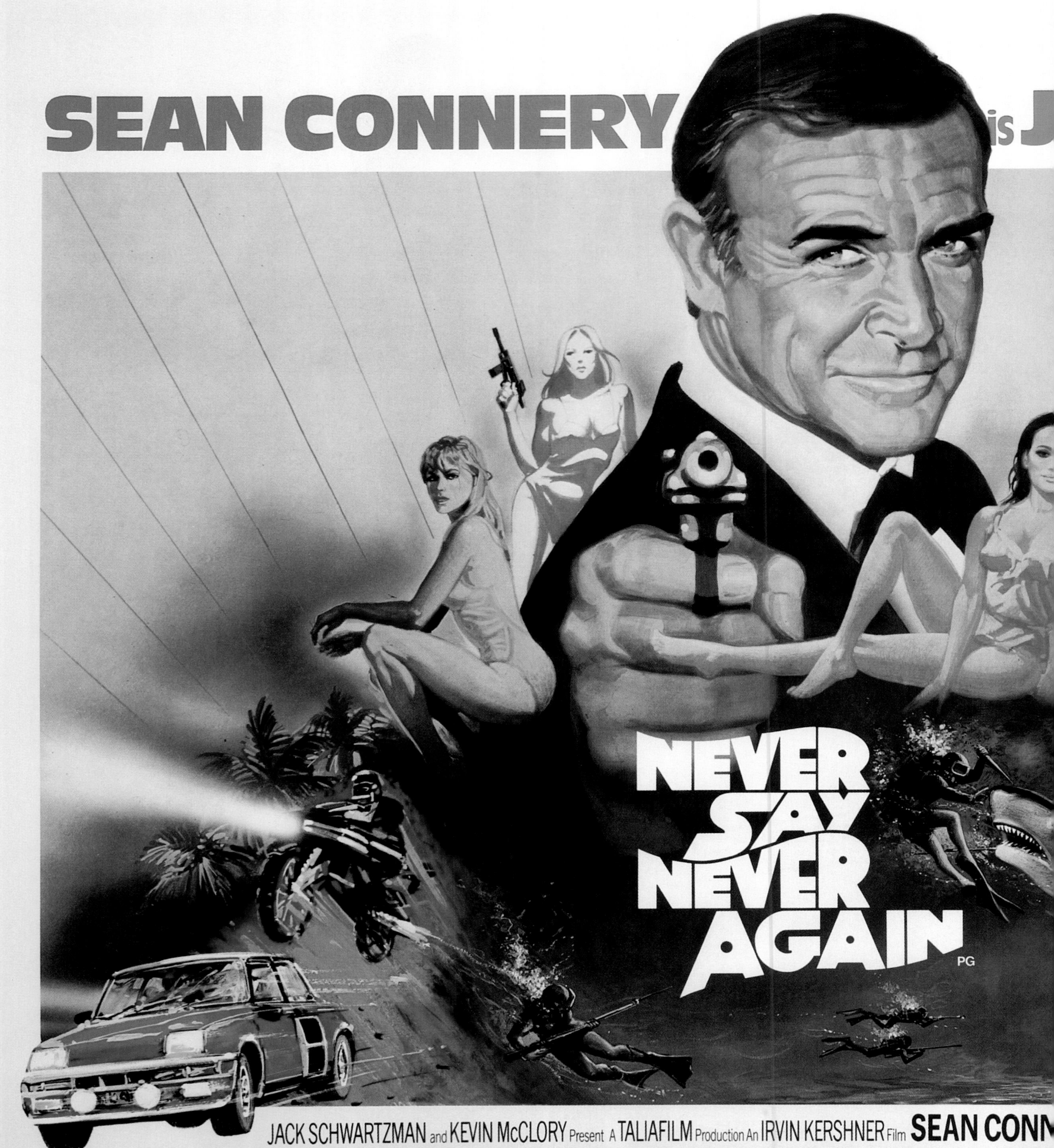
SEAN CONNERY is J
NEVER SAY NEVER AGAIN
PG
JACK SCHWARTZMAN and KEVIN McCLORY Present A TALIAFILM Production An IRVIN KERSHNER Film SEAN CONN
Also starring KLAUS MARIA BRANDAUER · MAX VON SYDOW · BARBARA CARRERA · KIM BASINGER · BERNIE CASEY · ALEC McCOWEN
Music by MICHEL LEGRAND Executive Producer KEVIN McCLORY Screenplay by LORENZO SEMPLE, JR. Based on an Original Story by KEVIN McCLORY, JACK WHITTINGHAM
Title song sung by LANI HALL Music by MICHEL LEGRAND Lyrics by ALAN and MARILYN BERGMAN
DOLBY STEREO IN SELECTED CINEMAS ONLY
Panavision® Technicolor®
DISTRIBUTED BY WARNER BROS

British 30 x 40 in (76 x 102 cm)

1984

Never Say Never Again

Following a twelve-year absence from the Bond films, a matured Sean Connery returned for this re-make of *Thunderball*. Following his legal battle with Ian Fleming, Kevin McClory had won the rights to produce this version of an already successful film, providing that he waited until after 1975. Audiences were generally unimpressed by, and perhaps harsh on, the older Connery.

Ernst Blofeld of the SPECTRE criminal organization has masterminded the theft of two nuclear warheads from a US Air Force base situated in the UK. When NATO is held to ransom, the main politicians give in and agree to pay up. While charming every woman in his path, Bond leaves a health farm and has to recover the warheads and capture the man who has stolen them, Largo, before the ransom is paid.

Renato Casaro painted the central image of Connery with a gun. This image, along with attractive illustrations of detailed action sequences, was used for the German campaign, while an alternative design featured the 007 logo repeated in the background. Variations on the main design were used for the different campaigns around the world.

German 33 x 23 in (84 x 58 cm)
Artist/Illustrator Renato Casaro
Date of release January 1984

Thai 37 x 26 in (94 x 65 cm)

JAMES BOND 007
กลับมาอย่างเต็มศักดิ์พยัคฆ์ร้าย!
"ฌอน" เป็น "บอนด์"
หลังจากหยุดไป 12 ปี
ทุนสร้าง 1500 ล้านบาท
เพื่อทำลายสถิติ "บอนด์" ทุกเรื่อง
ให้แหลกเป็นผุยผง!
007
พยัคฆ์เหนือพยัคฆ์
ฌอน คอนเนอรี่
บาบาร่า คาร์เรร่า
คิม บาซิงเกอร์
แม็กซ์ วอนไซโดว์
JACK SCHWARTZMAN and KEVIN McCLORY Present
A TALIAFILM Production · An IRVIN KERSHNER Film
SEAN CONNERY
NEVER SAY NEVER AGAIN
Also Starring KLAUS MARIA BRANDAUER · MAX VON SYDOW · BARBARA CARRERA · KIM BASINGER
BERNIE CASEY · ALEC McCOWEN and EDWARD FOX as "M" Director of Photography DOUGLAS SLOCOMBE B.S.C.
Music by MICHEL LEGRAND · Executive Producer KEVIN McCLORY · Screenplay by LORENZO SEMPLE, JR.
Based on a story by IAN FLEMING, KEVIN McCLORY and JACK WHITTINGHAM · Directed by IRVIN KERSHNER
Produced by JACK SCHWARTZMAN · Panavision® · Technicolor®
เป๊ปซี่
APEX
เอเพ็กซ์ภาพยนตร์
DOLBY STEREO
ฉายที่
วันที่

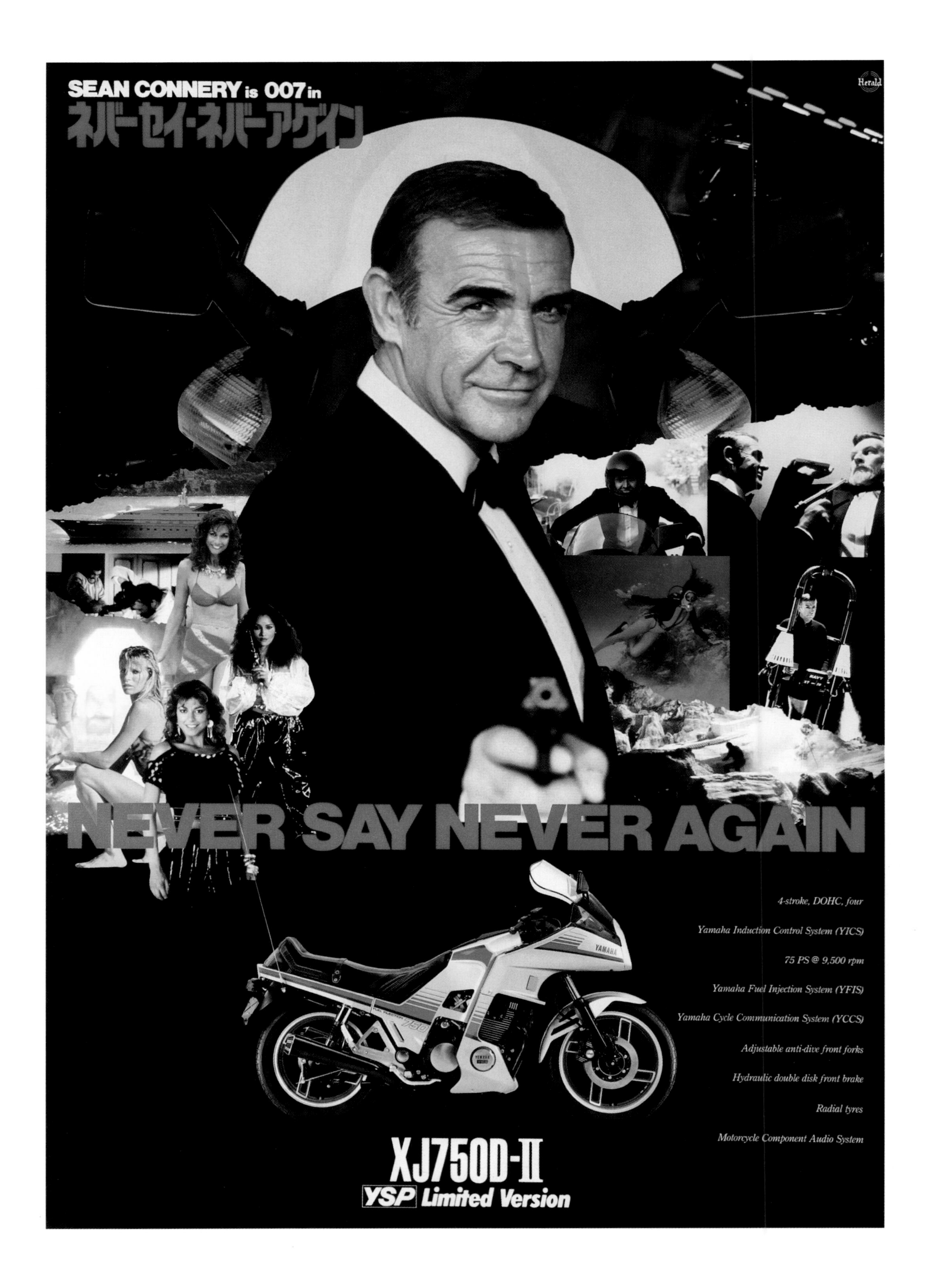

Japanese 28 x 20 in (71 x 51 cm)
(Special Yamaha tie-in)

Chinese 30 x 20 in (77 x 50 cm)

原庄「鉄金剛」
正牌「占士邦」
辛康納利
萬衆期待
東山復出之作
鐵金剛勇奪巡航導彈
「星球大戰」、「帝國反擊戰」大導演
艾榮卡舒納
★超水準傑作
「勝利大逃亡」大製片家
史和斯曼
★最新貢獻
SEAN CONNERY is 007 in
NEVER SAY NEVER AGAIN
Distributed by:
EASTERN FILMS ANSTALT
DELON INT'L FILM CORP.
廣告設計：
123電影廣告有限公司

Italian 39 x 27 in (99 x 69 cm)
(Gold lettering)
Translation: *Never Say Never*

US 41 x 27 in (104 x 69 cm)
(International)
Date of release October 1983

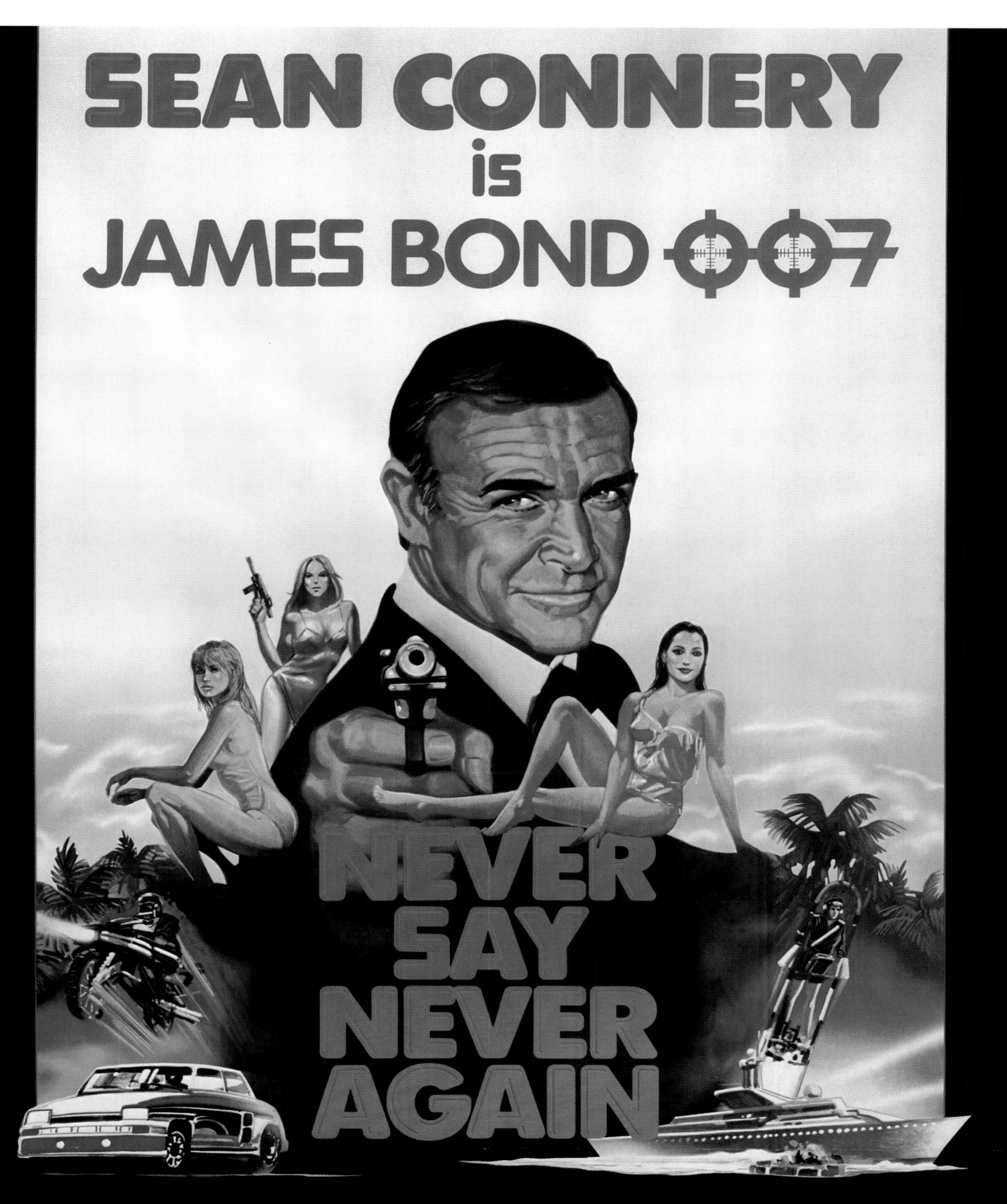
SEAN CONNERY
is
JAMES BOND 007
NEVER SAY NEVER AGAIN
KEVIN McCLORY and JACK SCHWARTZMAN Present
A TALIAFILM Production An IRVIN KERSHNER Film
SEAN CONNERY
"NEVER SAY NEVER AGAIN"
Also starring
KLAUS MARIA BRANDAUER · MAX VON SYDOW · BARBARA CARRERA · KIM BASINGER · BERNIE CASEY · ALEC McCOWEN and EDWARD FOX as "M"
Director of Photography DOUGLAS SLOCOMBE B.S.C. Music by MICHEL LEGRAND Executive Producer KEVIN McCLORY Screenplay by LORENZO SEMPLE, JR.
Based on an Original Story by KEVIN McCLORY, JACK WHITTINGHAM and IAN FLEMING Directed by IRVIN KERSHNER Produced by JACK SCHWARTZMAN
Title song sung by LANI HALL Music by MICHEL LEGRAND Lyrics by ALAN and MARILYN BERGMAN
DOLBY STEREO
Filmed in Panavision® Technicolor® Advertising © 1983 Taliafilm. All Rights Reserved.
From PARADISE FILM PRODUCTIONS II, LTD.

PSO
PRODUCERS
SALES
ORGANIZATION

1985
A View To A Kill

Roger Moore agreed to play Bond for a final time in *A View To A Kill*. The financial success of the Moore era indicates that the public approved both of Moore as a replacement for Sean Connery and also of his interpretation of the role. An amazing pre-credits sequence allowed the audience an insight into the impressive large-scale action scenes that would dominate the film. *A View To A Kill* has one of the most successful casts ever seen in a Bond film, with merciless villains such as Grace Jones and Oscar-winning Christopher Walken.

The British Secret Service suspect industrialist Max Zorin of leaking details of British microchip design to the Russians. With the help of Stacey Sutton, who had previously been pushed by Zorin to sell her late father's estate, Bond poses as a potential buyer of Zorin's horses and manages to gain access to Zorin's estate. Here the two learn of Zorin's plans to blow up Silicon Valley and so take control of the world's leading microchip market.

Illustrator Dan Gouzee was brought back for the second time to work on the campaign for *A View To A Kill* and created three different illustrations that were subsequently used worldwide. The illustration of Moore back to back with Grace Jones, with the tag line 'Has James Bond finally met his match?', ranks as one of the most striking images produced throughout the entire series. The other two images focused on the spectacular landmarks of the Eiffel Tower and the Golden Gate Bridge, where some breath-taking action sequences were filmed.

British 30 x 40 in (76 x 102 cm)
(Style A)
Artist/Illustrator Dan Gouzee
Date of release June 1985

Has JAMES BOND
finally met his match
ALBERT R. BROCCOLI Presents
ROGER MOORE
as IAN FLEMING'S
JAMES BOND 007
A VIEW TO A KILL PG
Starring TANYA ROBERTS · GRACE JONES ·
PATRICK MACNEE and CHRISTOPHER WALKEN
Music by JOHN BARRY
Production Designer PETER LAMONT
Associate Producer TOM PEVSNER
Produced by ALBERT R. BROCCOLI
and MICHAEL G. WILSON
Directed by JOHN GLEN
Screenplay by RICHARD MAIBAUM
and MICHAEL G. WILSON
ORIGINAL MOTION PICTURE SOUNDTRACK ON EMI RECORDS & TAPES
Title Song Performed by DURAN DURAN
PANAVISION®
DOLBY STEREO® IN SELECTED THEATRES
United Artists
TECHNICOLOR®
RELEASED BY MGM/UA ENTERTAINMENT CO.
© 1985 DANJAQ S.A. ALL RIGHTS RESERVED. © UIP 1985.
Distributed by UIP

This copyright advertising material is licensed and not sold and is the property of National Screen Service Ltd. and upon completion of the exhibition for which it has been licensed it should be returned to National Screen Service Ltd.

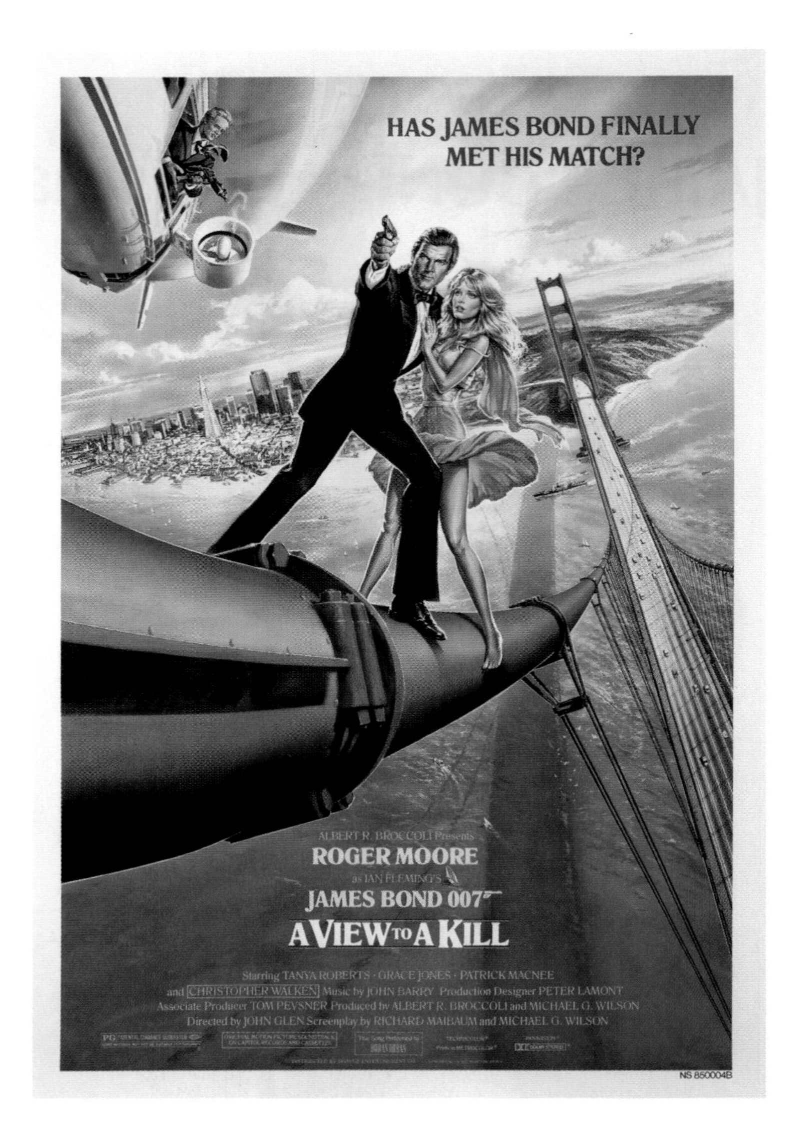

US 41 x 27 in (104 x 69 cm)
Artist/Illustrator Dan Gouzee
Date of release May 1985

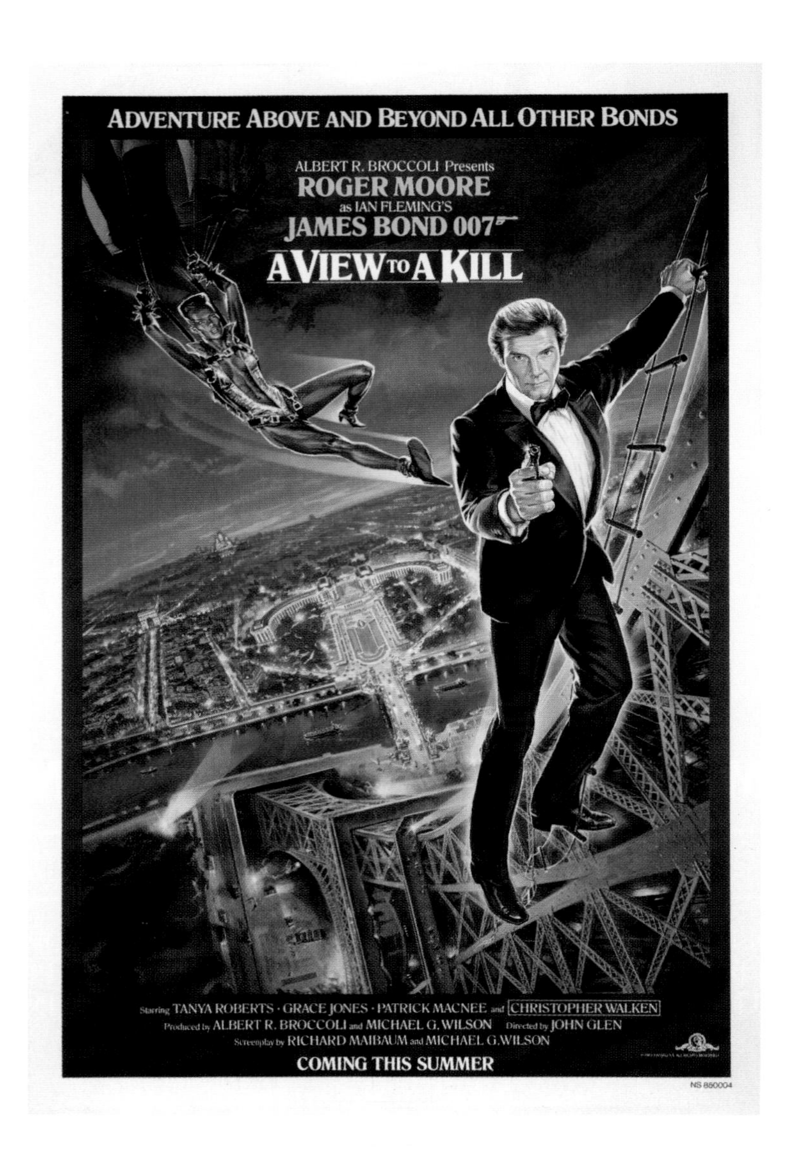

US 41 x 27 in (104 x 69 cm)
(Advance)
Artist/Illustrator Dan Gouzee

US 36 x 14 in (91 x 36 cm)
Artist/Illustrator Dan Gouzee

HAS JAMES BOND FINALLY
MET HIS MATCH?
ALBERT R. BROCCOLI Presents
ROGER MOORE
as IAN FLEMING'S
JAMES BOND 007
A VIEW TO A KILL
Starring TANYA ROBERTS · GRACE JONES · PATRICK MACNEE and CHRISTOPHER WALKEN
Music by JOHN BARRY Production Designer PETER LAMONT Associate Producer TOM PEVSNER
Produced by ALBERT R. BROCCOLI and MICHAEL G. WILSON Directed by JOHN GLEN
Screenplay by RICHARD MAIBAUM and MICHAEL G. WILSON
DOLBY STEREO
Title Song Performed by DURAN DURAN
ORIGINAL MOTION PICTURE SOUNDTRACK ON CAPITOL RECORDS AND CASSETTES
PANAVISION® TECHNICOLOR® Prints in METROCOLOR®
DISTRIBUTED BY MGM/UA ENTERTAINMENT CO.
850004

Japanese 28 x 20 in (71 x 51 cm)
(Style B)
Translation: *The Beautiful Prey*
Date of release July 1985

Japanese 28 x 20 in (71 x 51 cm)
(Style C)

ROGER MOORE
JAMES BOND 007
A VIEW TO A KILL
ボンド遂に史上最強の敵と対決。
シリーズ最新第14弾
007
美しき獲物たち
ロジャー・ムーア タニア・ロバーツ グレース・ジョーンズ クリストファー・ウォーケン
●製作アルバート・R・ブロッコリ ●監督ジョン・グレン ●音楽ジョン・バリー ●主題歌デュラン・デュラン
(サントラ盤 東芝EMI) ●原作イアン・フレミング〈カラー作品〉MGM映画 UIP配給

BOLLINGER®
The Champagne of James Bond 007
AS SEEN IN
A VIEW TO A KILL

Roger Moore as James Bond and Tanya Roberts as Stacey Sutton as seen in "A View to a Kill".
Bollinger Champagne Imported by The Buckingham Wile Company, New York, N.Y.
© 1985 Danjaq S.A. © MGM/UA Entertainment Co. 1985

US 36 x 24 in (91 x 61 cm)
(Bollinger tie-in)

US 49 x 33 in (124 x 84 cm)
(Michelin tie-in)

Michelin Dealers' 007 Sweepstakes

ADVENTURE ABOVE AND BEYOND ALL OTHER BONDS

ALBERT R. BROCCOLI Presents

ROGER MOORE

as IAN FLEMING'S

JAMES BOND 007

A VIEW TO A KILL

OPENING MAY 24TH AT A THEATER NEAR YOU.

Enter today for a chance to win one of these fabulous prizes!

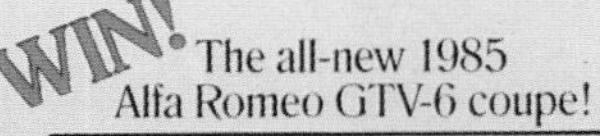

The all-new 1985 Alfa Romeo GTV-6 coupe!

A trip for two to New York!

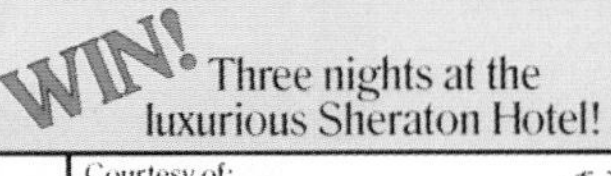

Three nights at the luxurious Sheraton Hotel!

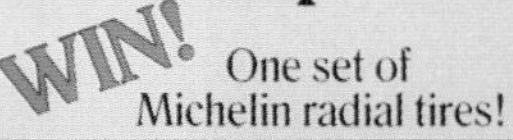

One set of Michelin radial tires!

Courtesy of:

The most passionately engineered cars in the world.

Courtesy of:

Courtesy of:

The Sheraton Centre & Towers New York
SHERATON HOTELS, INNS & RESORTS WORLDWIDE
7th AVENUE at 52nd STREET
NEW YORK, NY 10019
212/581-1000

Courtesy of:

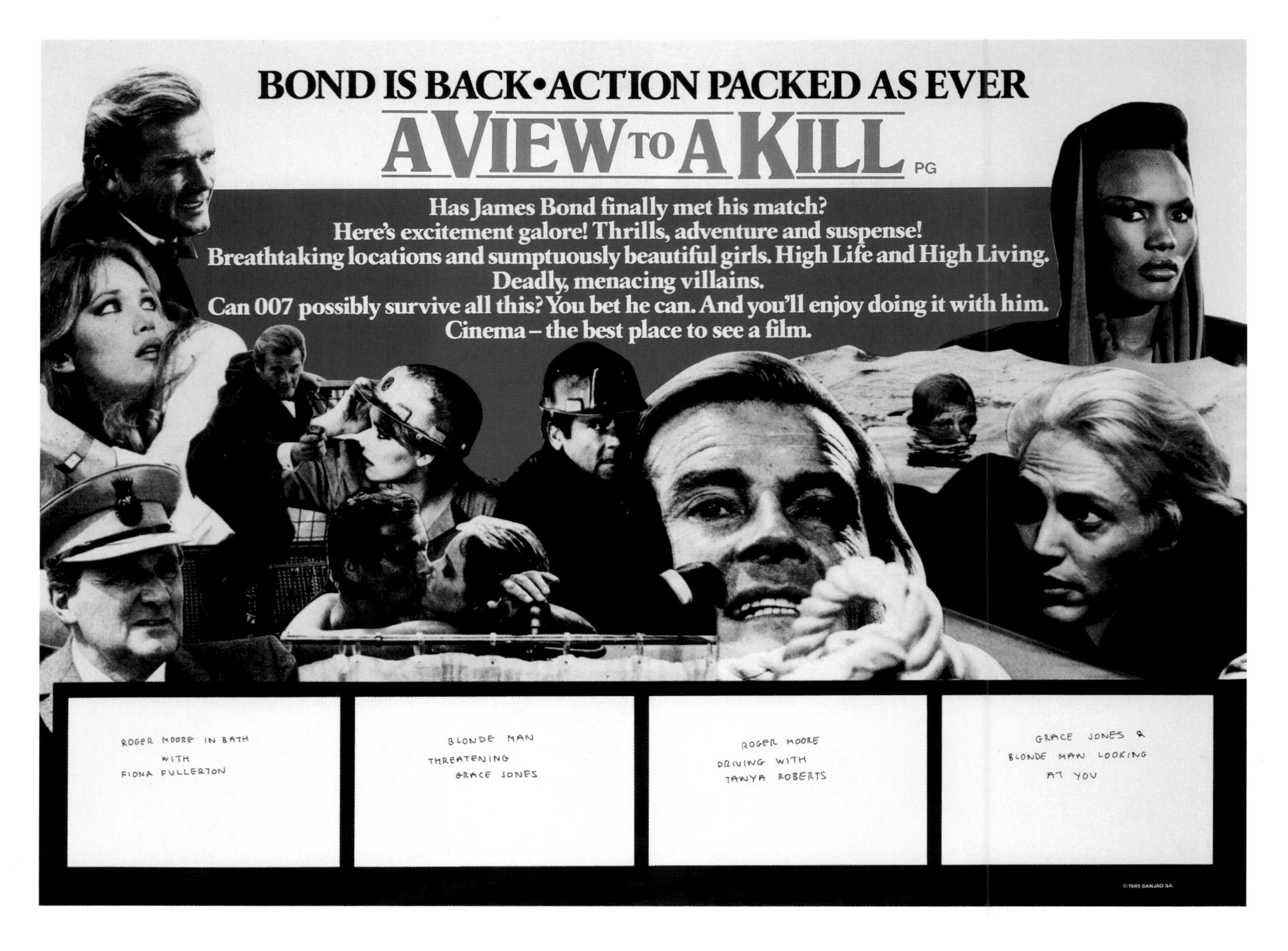

BOND IS BACK•ACTION PACKED AS EVER
A VIEW TO A KILL
PG
Has James Bond finally met his match?
Here's excitement galore! Thrills, adventure and suspense!
Breathtaking locations and sumptuously beautiful girls. High Life and High Living.
Deadly, menacing villains.
Can 007 possibly survive all this? You bet he can. And you'll enjoy doing it with him.
Cinema – the best place to see a film.
ROGER MOORE IN BATH WITH FIONA FULLERTON
BLONDE MAN THREATENING GRACE JONES
ROGER MOORE DRIVING WITH TANYA ROBERTS
GRACE JONES & BLONDE MAN LOOKING AT YOU

British 30 x 40 in (76 x 102 cm)

Cinemas were provided with film stills to be placed in the poster's blank squares. The 'blonde man' mentioned above would have been Christopher Walken.

British set of 4 each 30 x 20 in (76 x 51 cm)

A VIEW TO A KILL
PG
Smooth
operator

A VIEW TO A KILL
PG
Sinister
adversary
Deadly
beauty

007
ORIGINAL S
WEA RECOR
TECHNIC
Gun Logo Symbol ©

NEW JAMES BOND...
LIVING ON THE EDGE
ALBERT R. BROCCOLI
presents
TIMOTHY DALTON
as IAN FLEMING'S
AMES BOND 007
THE LIVING
DAYLIGHTS
PG
STARRING MARYAM d'ABO
JON BAKER ART MALIK AND JEROEN KRABBÉ
ON DESIGNER PETER LAMONT MUSIC BY JOHN BARRY
PRODUCERS TOM PEVSNER AND BARBARA BROCCOLI
BY ALBERT R. BROCCOLI AND MICHAEL G. WILSON
DIRECTED BY JOHN GLEN
Y BY RICHARD MAIBAUM AND MICHAEL G. WILSON
K ALBUM AVAILABLE ON
TES AND COMPACT DISC
ADDITIONAL SONGS PERFORMED BY
The Pretenders
TITLE SONG PERFORMED BY
a-ha
United Artists
DOLBY STEREO
Distributed by UNITED INTERNATIONAL PICTURES
© 1987 Danjaq, S.A. and United Artists Company. All Rights Reserved. © UIP 1987.

1987

The Living Daylights

Typically, the media created much hype over the choice of Timothy Dalton as the new 007. Bond fans appreciated his serious acting style and Dalton, in return, showed a darker side to Bond. The excellent cast, locations and score helped to make *The Living Daylights* a tremendous success, demonstrating to the world that Bond was still as popular as ever.

Soviet General Koskov informs MI6 of KGB General Pushkin's plans to kill all British agents. On further investigation, Bond learns that Koskov's story was a ploy to have Bond murder Pushkin, who was about to arrest Koskov for his criminal involvement with international arms dealer Brad Whitaker. Bond discovers that Koskov and Whitaker have been stealing Soviet money for an arms deal to finance the purchase of opium, which they can sell at huge profit.

The more serious and subtle approach that Timothy Dalton brought to the role ushered in a new era for Bond. However, the designers ensured that the link with Bond history was maintained. The famous image of Bond viewed through the end of a gun barrel was used in the international campaigns for *The Living Daylights*, so although audiences were faced by a new Bond, they were immediately put at ease by this familiar image. Bond was back, but still in the old, approved format.

British 30 x 40 in (76 x 102 cm)
Illustrator Brian Bysouth
Photographer Keith Hamshere
Date of release June 1987

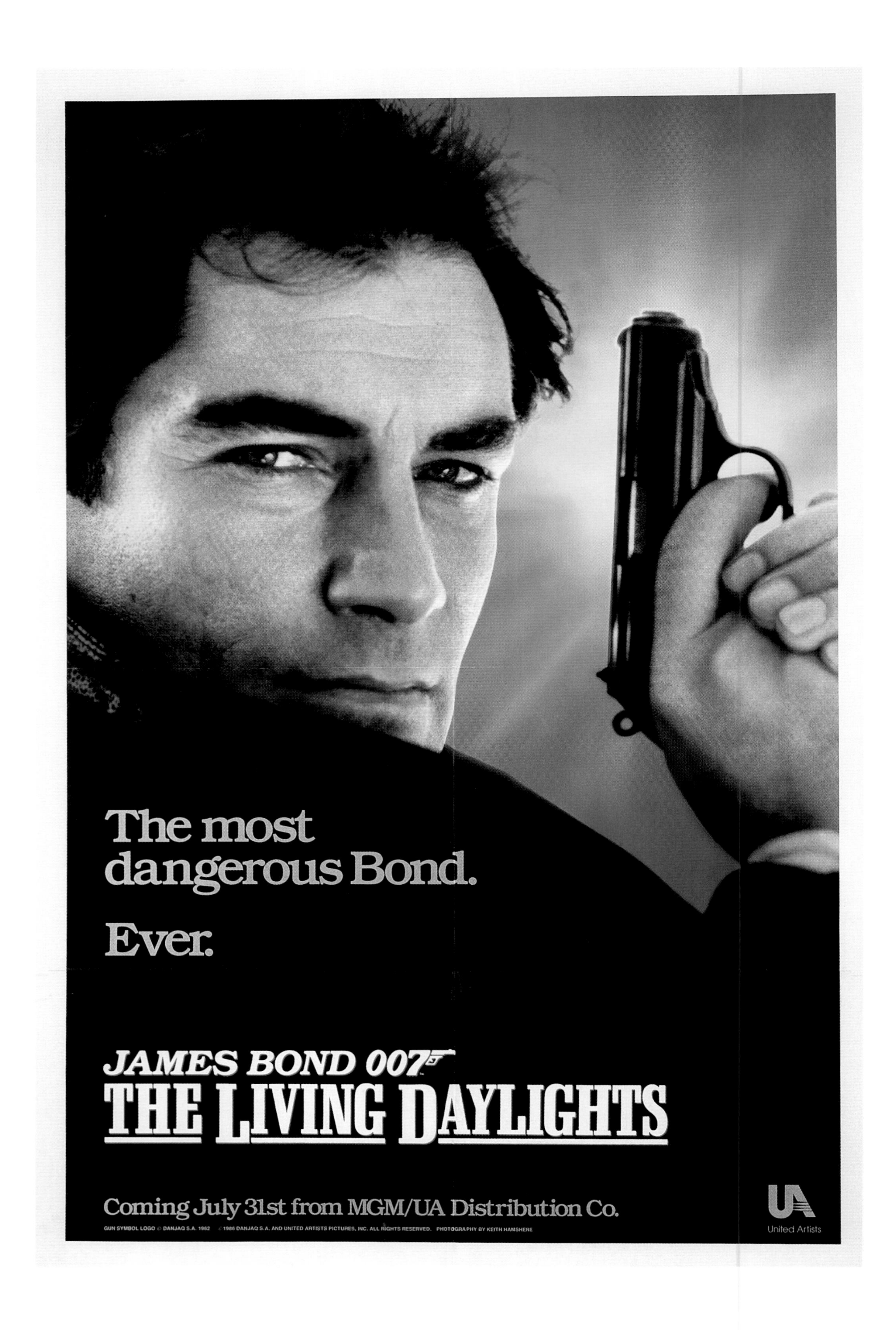

US 41 x 27 in (104 x 69 cm)
(Advance)
Photographer Keith Hamshere
Date of release July 1987

US 41 x 27 in (104 x 69 cm)
Art Direction & Designer Jeffrey Bacon
& David Reneric
Photographer Jim McCrary

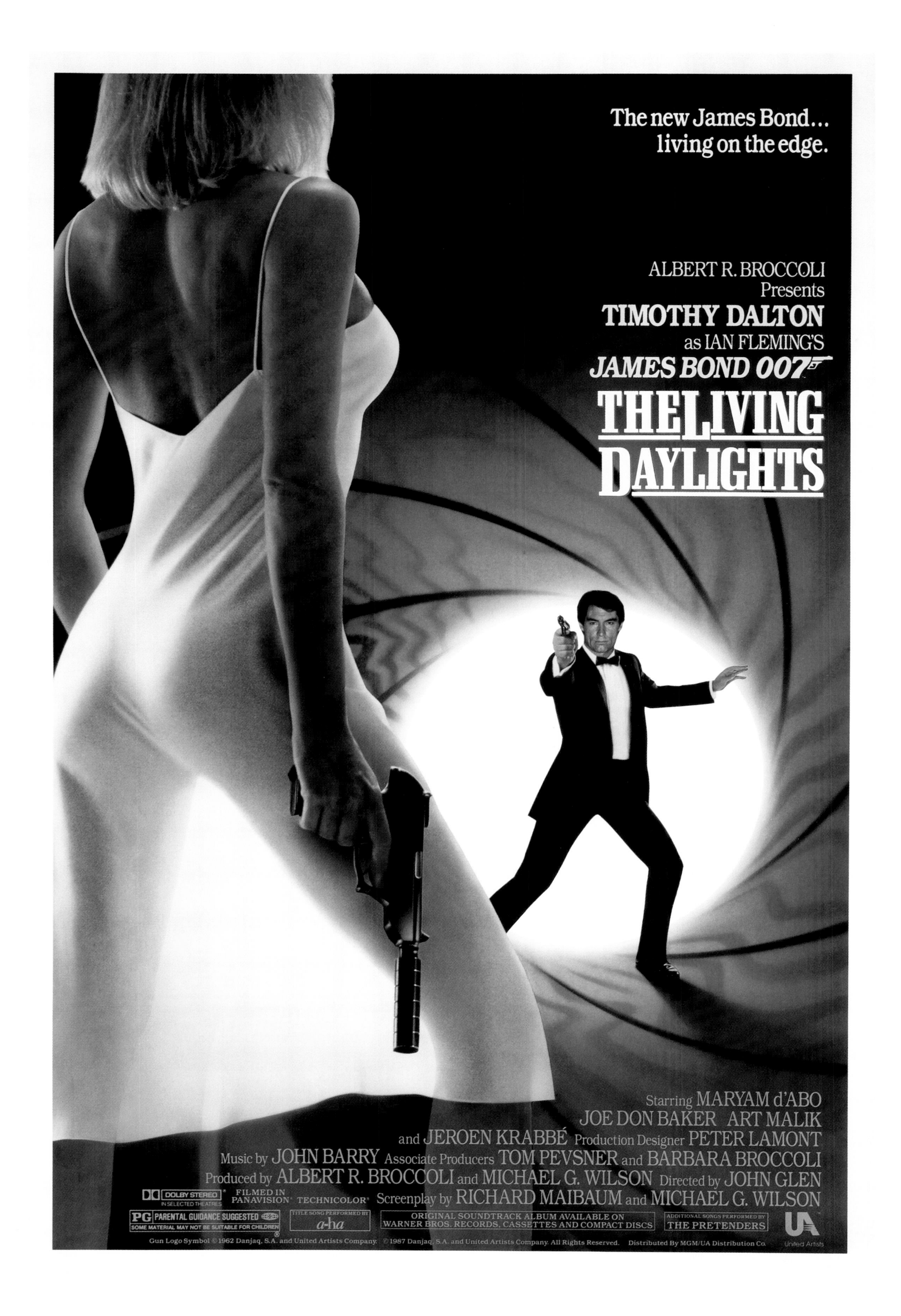
The new James Bond...
living on the edge.
ALBERT R. BROCCOLI
Presents
TIMOTHY DALTON
as IAN FLEMING'S
JAMES BOND 007
THE LIVING
DAYLIGHTS
Starring MARYAM d'ABO
JOE DON BAKER ART MALIK
and JEROEN KRABBÉ Production Designer PETER LAMONT
Music by JOHN BARRY Associate Producers TOM PEVSNER and BARBARA BROCCOLI
Produced by ALBERT R. BROCCOLI and MICHAEL G. WILSON Directed by JOHN GLEN
DOLBY STEREO
IN SELECTED THEATRES
FILMED IN PANAVISION
TECHNICOLOR
Screenplay by RICHARD MAIBAUM and MICHAEL G. WILSON
PG PARENTAL GUIDANCE SUGGESTED
SOME MATERIAL MAY NOT BE SUITABLE FOR CHILDREN
TITLE SONG PERFORMED BY
a-ha
ORIGINAL SOUNDTRACK ALBUM AVAILABLE ON
WARNER BROS. RECORDS, CASSETTES AND COMPACT DISCS
ADDITIONAL SONGS PERFORMED BY
THE PRETENDERS
UA
United Artists
Gun Logo Symbol © 1962 Danjaq, S.A. and United Artists Company. © 1987 Danjaq, S.A. and United Artists Company. All Rights Reserved. Distributed By MGM/UA Distribution Co.

US 28 x 20 in (71 x 51 cm)
(Advance Carlsberg tie-in)

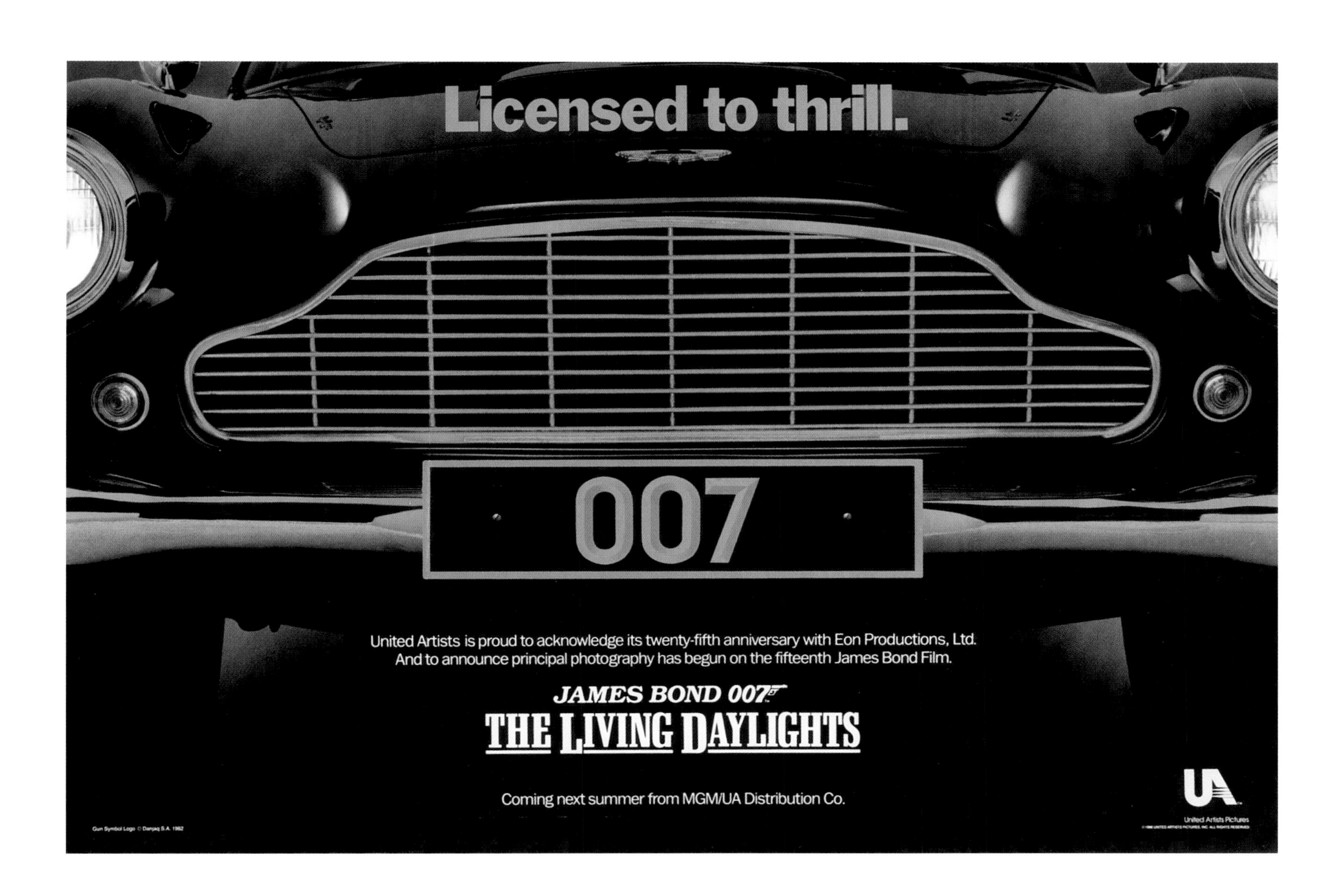

US 12 x 17 in (30 x 44 cm)
(Advance)

James Bond is out on his own
and out for revenge

ALBERT R. BROCCOLI
presents
TIMOTHY DALTON
as IAN FLEMING'S
JAMES BOND 007
LICENCE TO KI

STARRING CAREY LOWELL ROBERT DAVI TALISA SOTO ANTHONY ZER
DIRECTOR OF PHOTOGRAPHY ALEC MILLS PRODUCTION DESIGNER PETER LAMONT MUSIC BY MICHAEL KAMEN ASSOCIATE PRODUCERS TOM PEVSNER
WRITTEN BY MICHAEL G. WILSON AND RICHARD MAIBAUM PRODUCED BY ALBERT R. BROCCOLI AND MICHAEL G.
DISTRIBUTED BY UNITED INTERNATIONAL PICTURES SPECTRAL RECORDING DOLBY STEREO SR IN SELECTED THEATRES FILMED IN PANAVISION® COLOUR BY DELUXE® PRINTS BY TECHNICOLOR® Original Motion Picture Soundtrack

1989

Licence To Kill

The Dalton era ended with *Licence To Kill*, after a brief but popular return of the serious espionage thriller. The well-written screenplay told of Bond pursuing a personal vengeance, and was to be more violent, and more realistic, than its predecessors. This foray into the mature action-adventure market, inviting competition from such blockbusters as *Batman* and *Indiana Jones And The Last Crusade*, resulted in lower box-office grosses for Bond than was the norm. This left cynics suggesting that *Licence To Kill* marked the end of the pop era icon.

On CIA Agent Felix Leiter's wedding day, he and his best man Bond capture Franz Sanchez, a notorious drug baron. However, Sanchez escapes and seeks revenge by mutilating Felix and murdering his new wife. A determined and angry Bond ignores M's order to leave matters alone and embarks on a worldwide personal vendetta against Sanchez, temporarily leaving Her Majesty's Secret Service.

The original title for this film had been '*Licence Revoked*' and at an early stage Bob Peak was hired to provide the illustrations for the campaign. Unfortunately when the title changed, his designs – despite having the backing of Cubby Broccoli – were ultimately turned down in favour of what might be considered a less inspiring design.

British 30 x 40 in (76 x 102 cm)
Art Director Robin Behling
Date of release June 1989

007
ALBERT R. BROCCOLI
Presents
TIMOTHY DALTON
as IAN FLEMING'S
JAMES BOND 007
LICENCE TO KILL
Starring CAREY LOWELL ROBERT DAVI TALISA SOTO ANTHONY ZERBE
Director of Photography ALEC MILLS Production Designer PETER LAMONT Music by MICHAEL KAMEN
Associate Producers TOM PEVSNER and BARBARA BROCCOLI Written by MICHAEL G. WILSON and RICHARD MAIBAUM
Produced by ALBERT R. BROCCOLI and MICHAEL G. WILSON Directed by JOHN GLEN
PG-13 PARENTS STRONGLY CAUTIONED
Some Material May Be Inappropriate for Children Under 13
Filmed in PANAVISION® Color by DELUXE® Prints by TECHNICOLOR®
ORIGINAL MOTION PICTURE SOUNDTRACK ALBUM ON MCA RECORDS, CASSETTES AND COMPACT DISCS
DOLBY STEREO SR
UA
890005
LICENSE TO KILL

US 41 x 27 in (104 x 69 cm)
Photographers Keith Hamshere & Douglas Kirkland
Designer Tony Synegar
Date of release July 1989

US 41 x 27 in (104 x 69 cm)
(Advance)
Photographer Keith Hamshere

His bad side is
a dangerous
place to be.
TIMOTHY DALTON
JAMES BOND 007
LICENCE TO KILL
COMING JULY '89
UA
Gun Logo Symbol ©1962 Danjaq, S.A. and United Artists Company.
© 1988 Danjaq, S.A. and United Artists Company. All Rights Reserved. Distributed by MGM/UA Distribution Co.
United Artists

British 60 x 20 in (152 x 51 cm)
Photographer Keith Hamshere
(Style A)

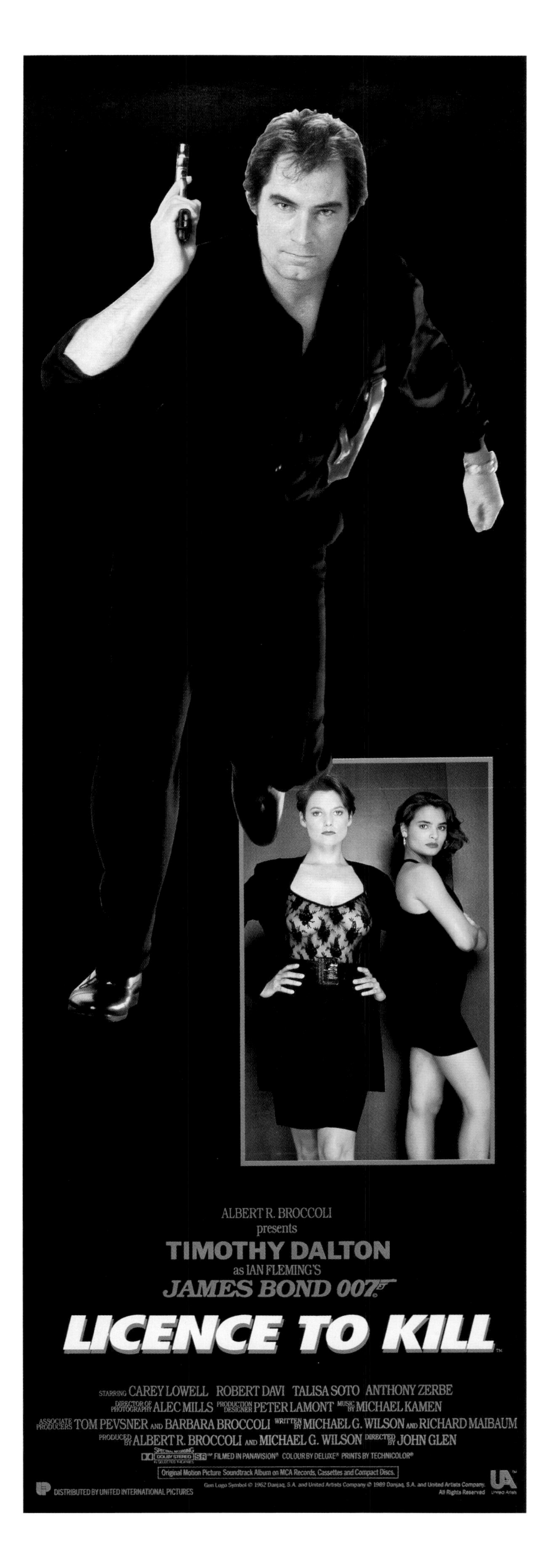

British 60 x 20 in (152 x 51 cm)
Photographers Keith Hamshere
& Douglas Kirkland
(Style B)

1995
GoldenEye

The next Bond film had to wait six years to see the light of day, due to heavy litigation between Eon and MGM/United Artists. Nevertheless, Cubby Broccoli was keen to see the return of James Bond. However, when Timothy Dalton announced his departure from the role, Eon was left with a crisis and had to find yet another 007. Pierce Brosnan had missed an opportunity to take the role in 1986, and he was keen not to let it happen again. Those few extra years had perhaps made Brosnan more suitable than ever to play the part of Bond, a character who had survived the modern world and retained an old-fashioned air of style and grace. The old team was reassembled and a new studio was built especially for the production. Barbara Broccoli joined Michael Wilson as producer, and together they took the series to new box-office heights. The astounding box-office figures confirmed to the world that, indeed, Bond was back.

Bond's mission is to steal back a top-secret space weapon called the GoldenEye. In the wrong hands, this satellite could destroy all the electronic equipment within a specified target area. 007 learns that the weapon is in the control of Alec Trevelyan, a former colleague and British agent, who had been reported killed nine years earlier. He must stop Trevelyan, who has major plans to financially cripple London.

A bold and modern poster campaign was created, which adapted effortlessly to its nineties setting without sacrificing its traditional Bondian roots. However, the original US advance poster was rejected, because the image of the gun barrel pointing directly at the spectator was not acceptable for use in certain territories (for example, the London underground prohibits the use of such images). The preferred US advance poster stated boldly 'You know the name, you know the number' – indeed, audiences could hardly have forgotten, despite the lengthy gap between Bond films.

British 30 x 40 in (76 x 102 cm)
Photographers Terry O'Neil, Keith Hamshere & George Whitear
Art Directors Earl Klasky & Randi Braun
Date of release November 1995

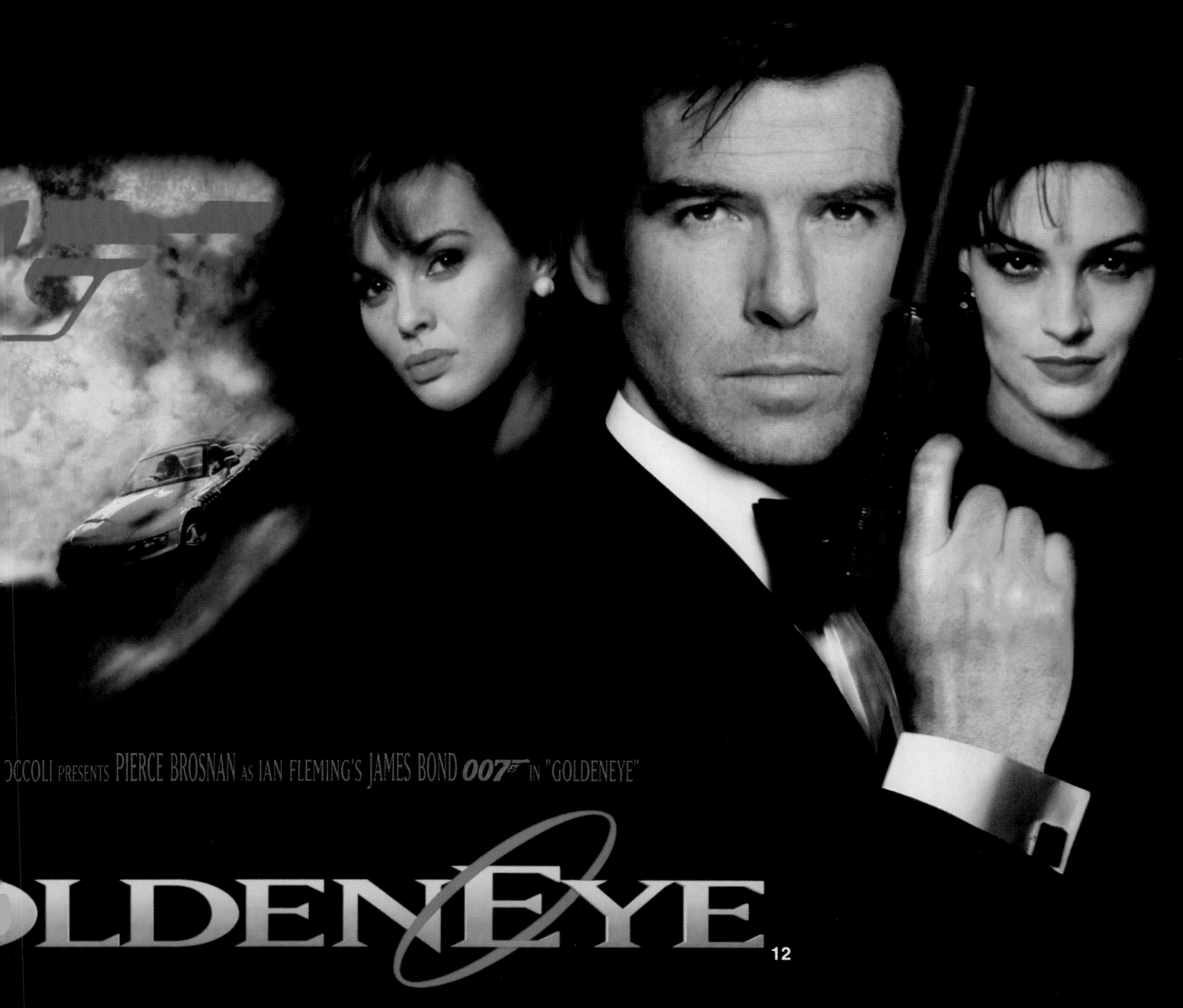
No fears. No substitutes.
PRESENTS PIERCE BROSNAN AS IAN FLEMING'S JAMES BOND 007 IN "GOLDENEYE"
LDENEYE
12
'S JAMES BOND 007 IN "GOLDENEYE" SEAN BEAN IZABELLA SCORUPCO FAMKE JANSSEN AND JOE DON BAKER MUSIC BY ERIC SERRA
TOM PEVSNER STORY BY MICHAEL FRANCE SCREENPLAY BY JEFFREY CAINE AND BRUCE FEIRSTEIN PRODUCED BY MICHAEL G. WILSON AND BARBARA BROCCOLI DIRECTED BY MARTIN CAMPBELL
WRITTEN BY BONO AND THE EDGE PERFORMED BY TINA TURNER
INTERNET ADDRESS http://www.uip.com
DOLBY
dts
UNITED ARTISTS
An MGM Company

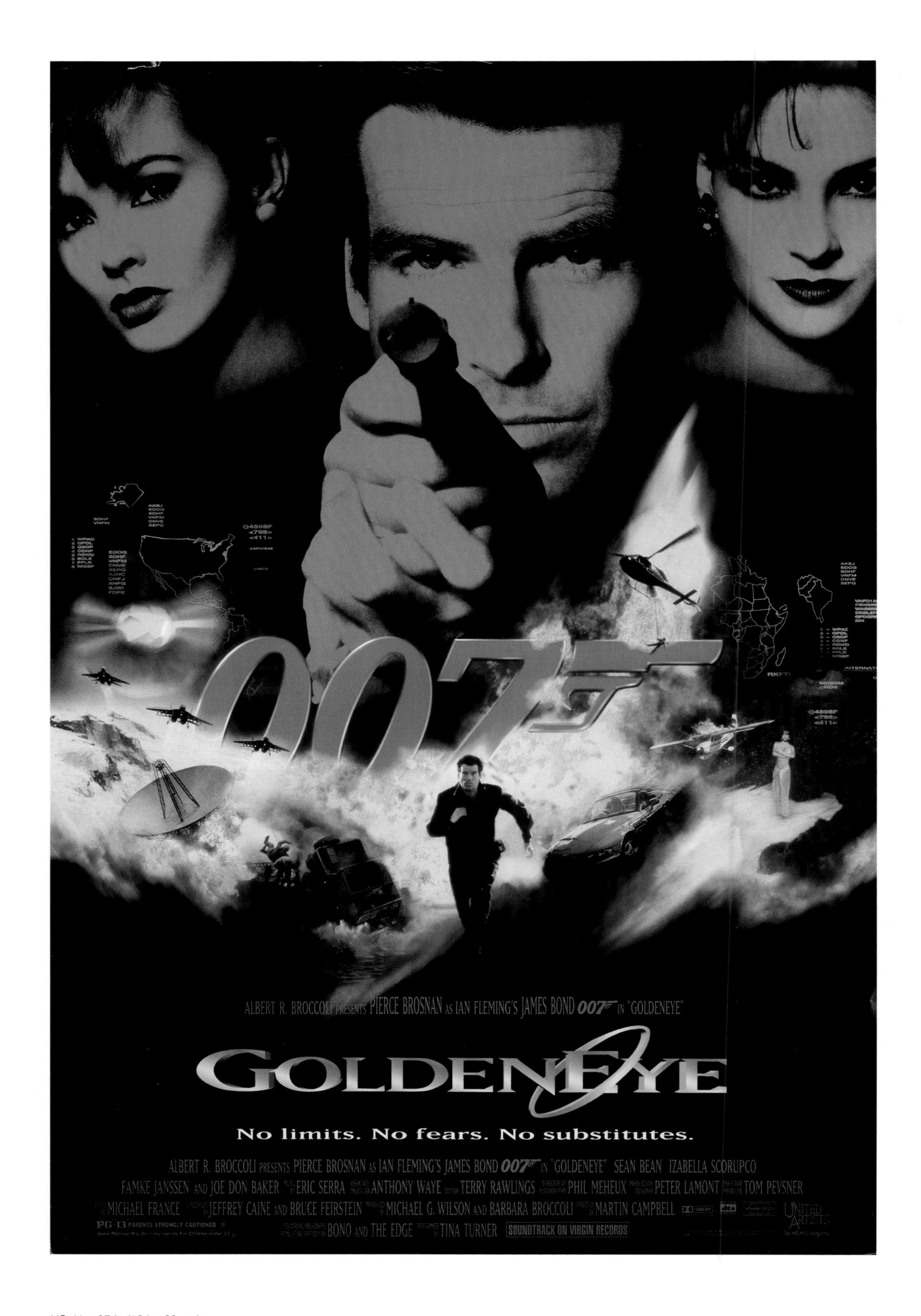

US 41 x 27 in (104 x 69 cm)
Photographers Terry O'Neil, Keith Hamshere & George Whitear
Art Director Earl Klasky & Randi Braun
Date of release November 1995

US 41 x 27 in (104 x 69 cm)
(Advance)
Photographer Terry O'Neil
Art Director Earl Klasky & Randi Braun

THERE IS NO SUBSTITUTE
007™
ALBERT R. BROCCOLI PRESENTS PIERCE BROSNAN AS JAMES BOND 007 IN "GOLDENEYE" SEAN BEAN IZABELLA SCORUPCO FAMKE JANSSEN AND JOE DON BAKER ASSOCIATE PRODUCER ANTHONY WAYE EDITOR TERRY RAWLINGS
DIRECTOR OF PHOTOGRAPHY PHIL MEHEUX PRODUCTION DESIGNER PETER LAMONT EXECUTIVE PRODUCER TOM PEVSNER WRITTEN BY MICHAEL FRANCE AND JEFFREY CAINE PRODUCED BY MICHAEL G. WILSON AND BARBARA BROCCOLI DIRECTED BY MARTIN CAMPBELL
CHRISTMAS '95

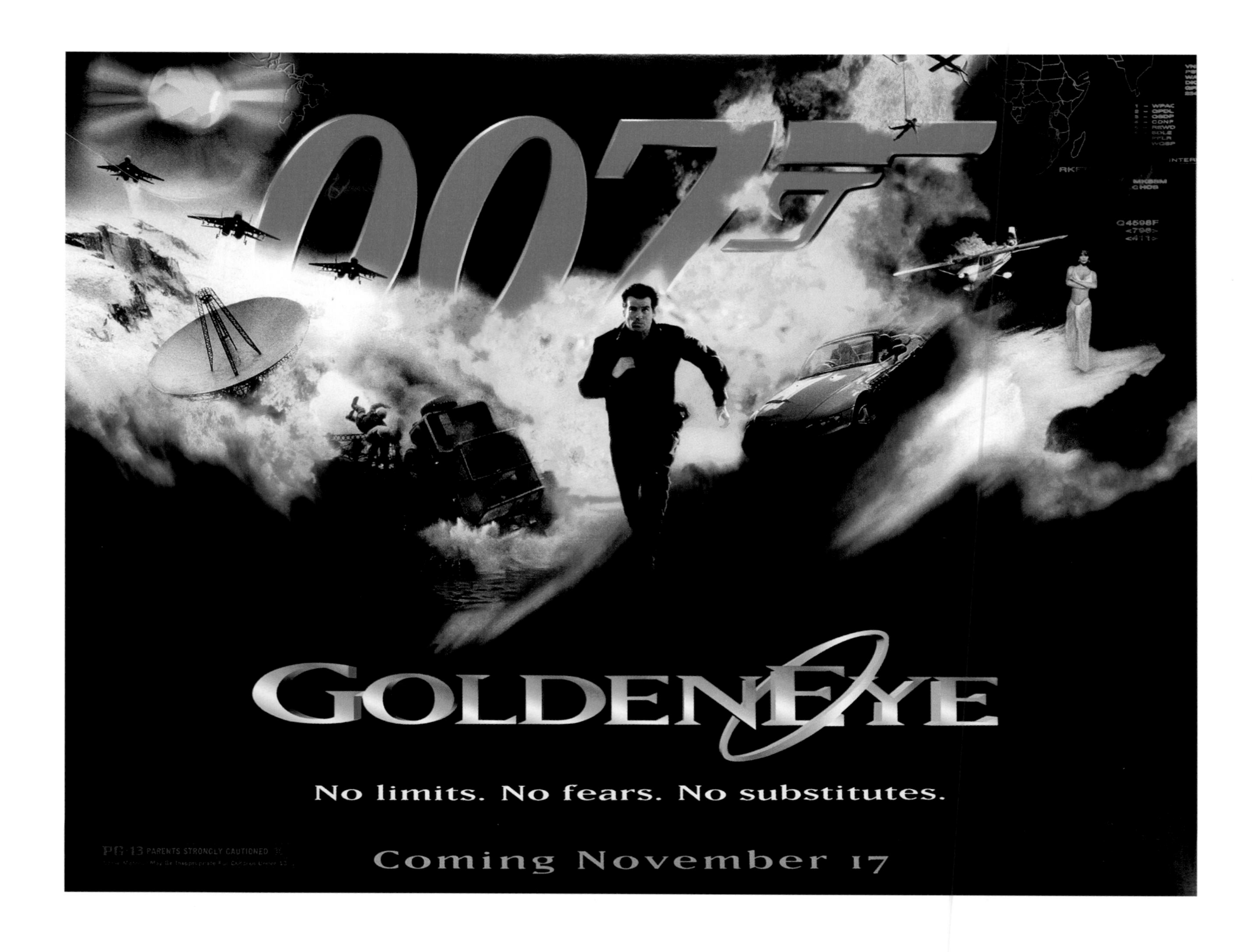

British 30 x 40 in (76 x 102 cm)
(Advance)
Photographers Keith Hamshere & George Whitear
Art Directors Earl Klasky & Randi Braun

Japanese 40 x 29 in (102 x 74 cm)
(Advance)
Photographer Terry O'Neil
Date of release December 1995

You know the name
You know the number

007™

新しい世界——

ゴールデンアイ

UNITED
INTERNATIONAL
PICTURES

UNITED
ARTISTS™

1997

Tomorrow Never Dies

The production of *Tomorrow Never Dies* was beset by numerous difficulties, not least having to build another studio from scratch and switching the film's Vietnam locations to Thailand at the last minute. Nevertheless, Brosnan returned to the role, his screen charisma doing much to ensure the success of this, his second Bond outing. Combining an up-to-the-minute hi-tech film with the classic elements of fabulous women, gadgets and spectacular action sequences, the classic Bondian recipe was still proven to work.

Megalomaniac media tycoon Elliot Carver has created an ingenious scheme to secure a monopoly over the news industry. He plans to instigate catastrophic international disasters and ensure that his reporters are at the scene first. But Carver ultimately aims to go one step further, and use his technology to bring about a nuclear war between Britain and China. Bond has to beat the clock and prevent what could result in World War III.

Following the huge success of *GoldenEye*, Brosnan became instantly recognizable to international audiences. The main campaign showed a simple image of Brosnan in two different poses, surrounded by the familiar gun-barrel. The poster campaign adopted a modern approach again, using the recently adapted logo and television screens to reflect the media-based storyline.

British 30 x 40 in (76 x 102 cm)
Art Director Randi Braun
Photographers Keith Hamshere & George Whitear
Date of release December 1997

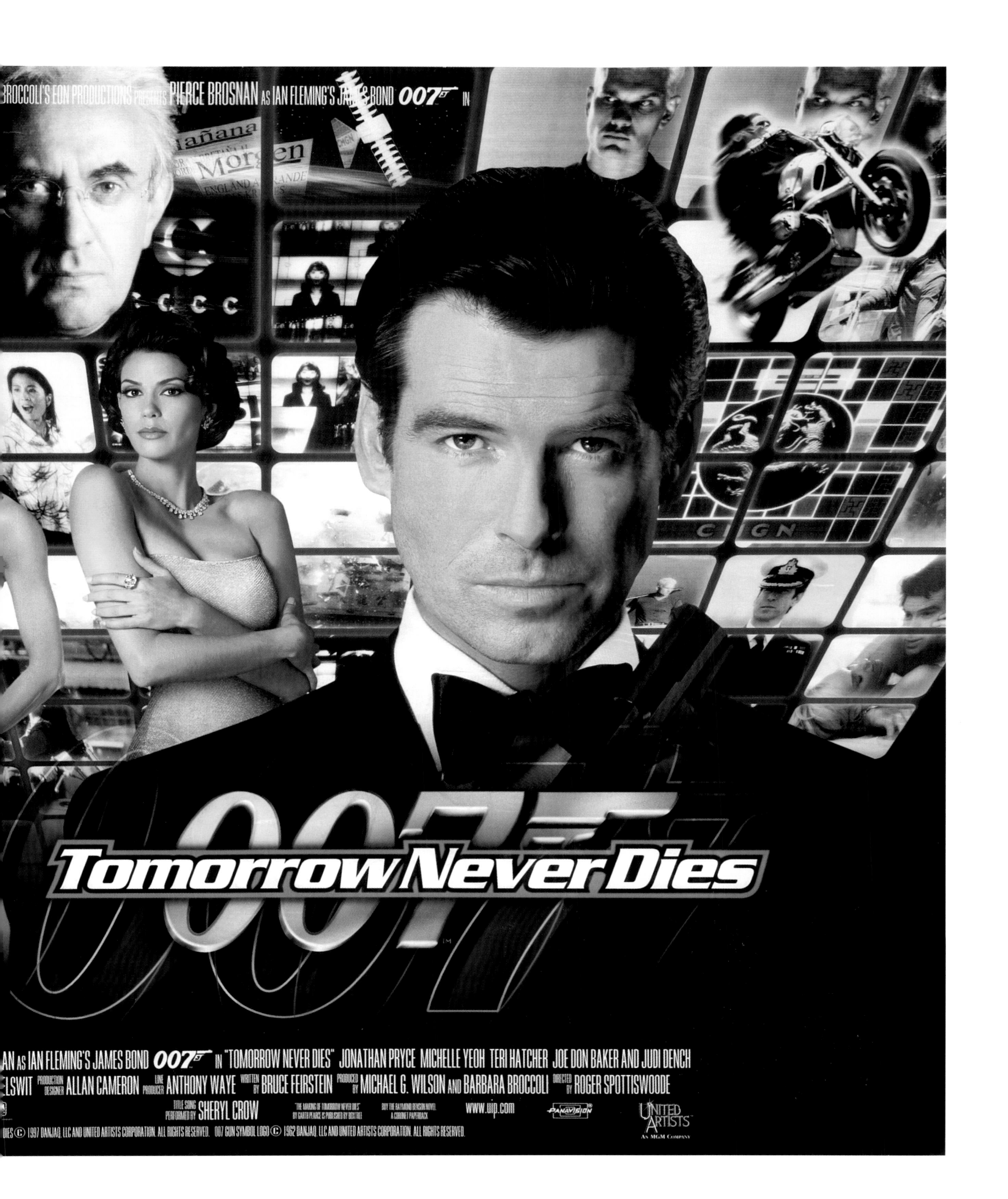
EON PRODUCTIONS PRESENTS PIERCE BROSNAN AS IAN FLEMING'S
BOND 007 IN
Mañana
Morgen
007
Tomorrow Never Dies
AS IAN FLEMING'S JAMES BOND 007 IN "TOMORROW NEVER DIES" JONATHAN PRYCE MICHELLE YEOH TERI HATCHER JOE DON BAKER AND JUDI DENCH
PRODUCTION DESIGNER ALLAN CAMERON LINE PRODUCER ANTHONY WAYE WRITTEN BY BRUCE FEIRSTEIN PRODUCED BY MICHAEL G. WILSON AND BARBARA BROCCOLI DIRECTED BY ROGER SPOTTISWOODE
TITLE SONG PERFORMED BY SHERYL CROW
www.uip.com
PANAVISION
UNITED ARTISTS
AN MGM COMPANY
© 1997 DANJAQ, LLC AND UNITED ARTISTS CORPORATION. ALL RIGHTS RESERVED. 007 GUN SYMBOL LOGO © 1962 DANJAQ, LLC AND UNITED ARTISTS CORPORATION. ALL RIGHTS RESERVED.

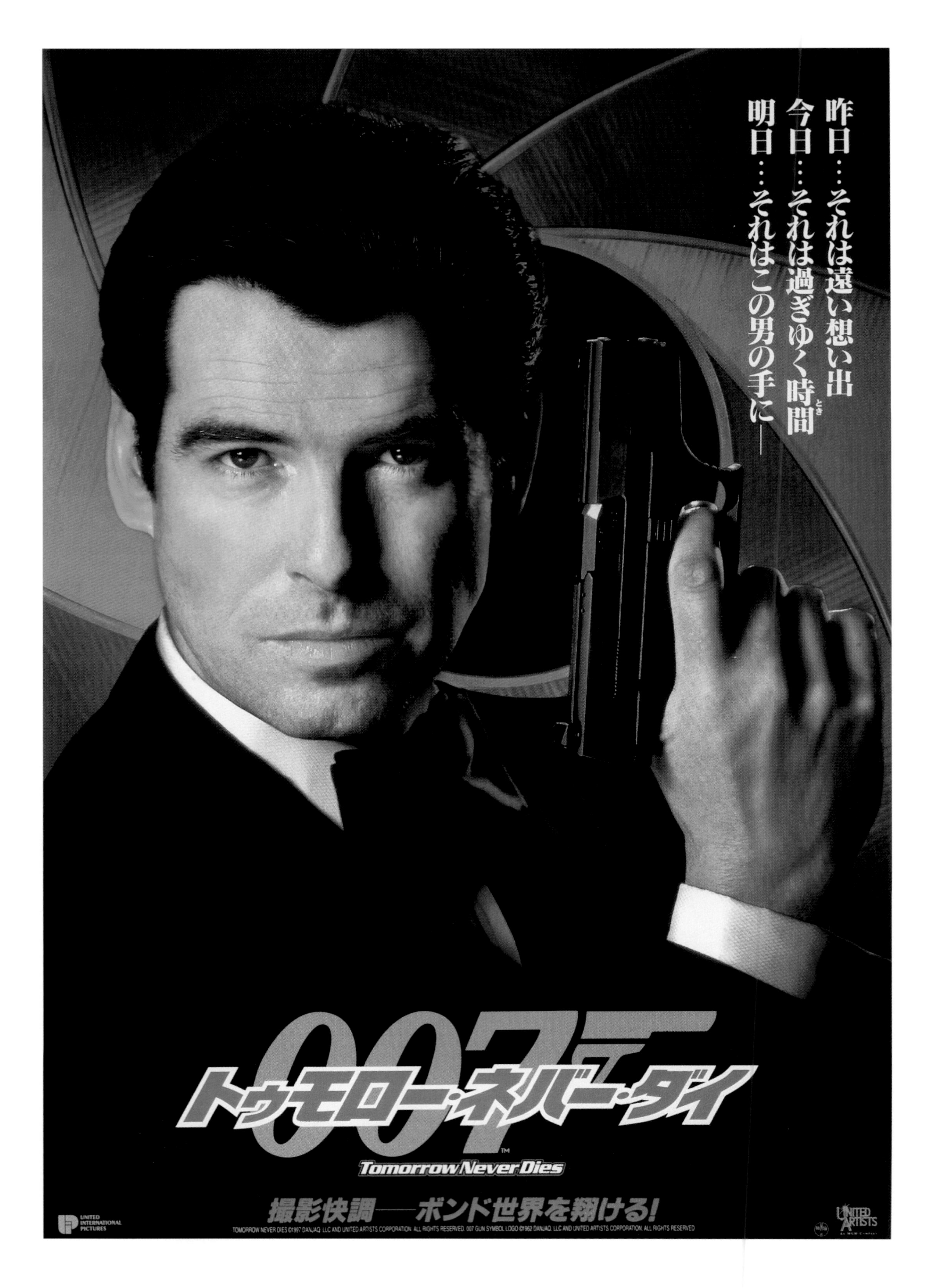

Japanese 28 x 20 in (71 x 51 cm)
(Advance)
Photographer Keith Hamshere
Date of release March 1998

Japanese 28 x 20 in (71 x 51 cm)
(Advance Style B)

アルバート・R・ブロッコリ/イオン・プロダクション提供 ピアース・ブロスナン=イアン・フレミング原案 ジェームズ・ボンド 007
MEET NEW JAMES BOND
007
Tomorrow Never Dies
トゥモロー・ネバー・ダイ
アルバート・R・ブロッコリ/イオン・プロダクション提供 ピアース・ブロスナン=イアン・フレミング原案 ジェームズ・ボンド 007 IN "TOMORROW NEVER DIES"
ジョナサン・プライス ミシェル・ヨー テリー・ハッチャー ジョー・ドン・ベイカーANDジュディ・デンチ 衣装デザイン:リンディ・ヘミング 音楽:デビッド・アーノルド 撮影:ロバート・エルスウィット プロダクション・デザイナー:アラン・キャメロン ライン・プロデューサー:アンソニー・ウェイ
脚本:ブルース・フィアステイン 製作:マイケル・G・ウィルソンANDバーバラ・ブロッコリ 監督:ロジャー・スポティスウッド UIP配給/ユナイテッド・アーチスツ映画
UNITED INTERNATIONAL PICTURES
DOLBY
www.uip.com
サントラ/主題歌:シェリル・クロウ(ポリドール) ノベライゼーション:角川文庫刊
PANAVISION
UNITED ARTISTS

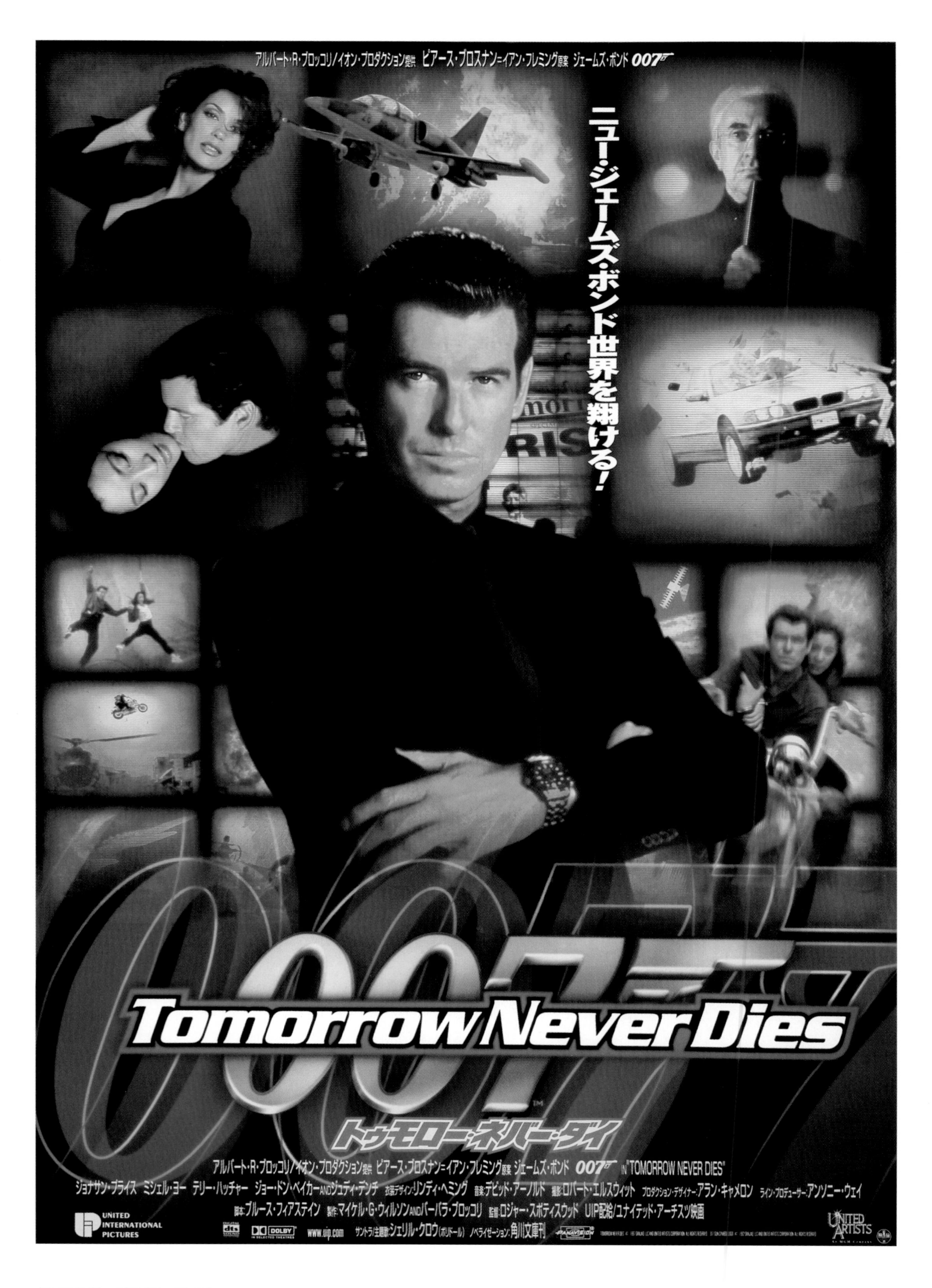

Japanese 28 x 20 in (71 x 51 cm)
Photographer Keith Hamshere
(Style B)

US 41 x 27 in (104 x 69 cm)
Date of release December 1997

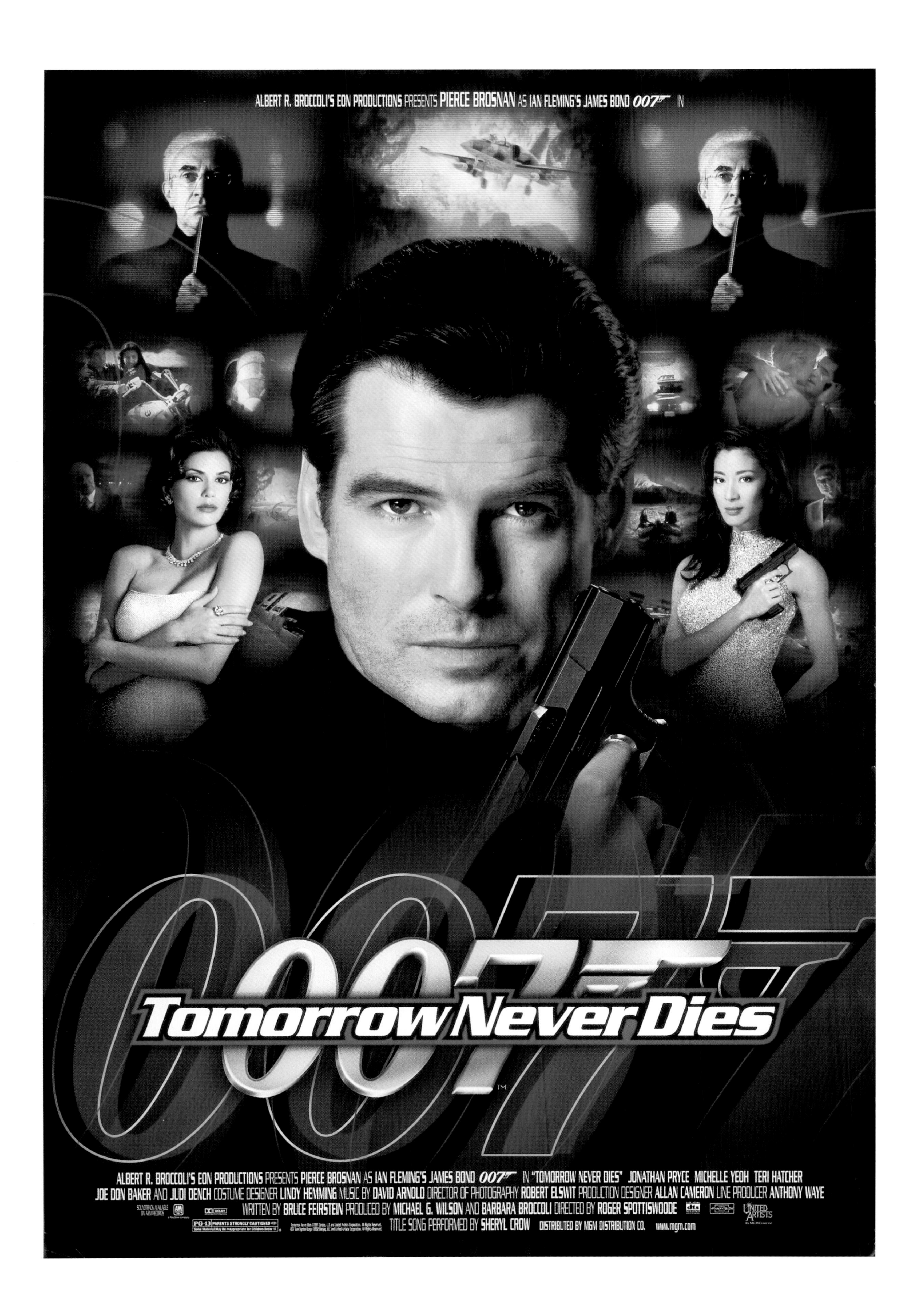
ALBERT R. BROCCOLI'S EON PRODUCTIONS PRESENTS PIERCE BROSNAN AS IAN FLEMING'S JAMES BOND 007 IN
007
Tomorrow Never Dies
ALBERT R. BROCCOLI'S EON PRODUCTIONS PRESENTS PIERCE BROSNAN AS IAN FLEMING'S JAMES BOND 007 IN "TOMORROW NEVER DIES" JONATHAN PRYCE MICHELLE YEOH TERI HATCHER
JOE DON BAKER AND JUDI DENCH COSTUME DESIGNER LINDY HEMMING MUSIC BY DAVID ARNOLD DIRECTOR OF PHOTOGRAPHY ROBERT ELSWIT PRODUCTION DESIGNER ALLAN CAMERON LINE PRODUCER ANTHONY WAYE
WRITTEN BY BRUCE FEIRSTEIN PRODUCED BY MICHAEL G. WILSON AND BARBARA BROCCOLI DIRECTED BY ROGER SPOTTISWOODE
PG-13 PARENTS STRONGLY CAUTIONED
TITLE SONG PERFORMED BY SHERYL CROW
DISTRIBUTED BY MGM DISTRIBUTION CO.
www.mgm.com
UNITED ARTISTS

The
V354 FMP

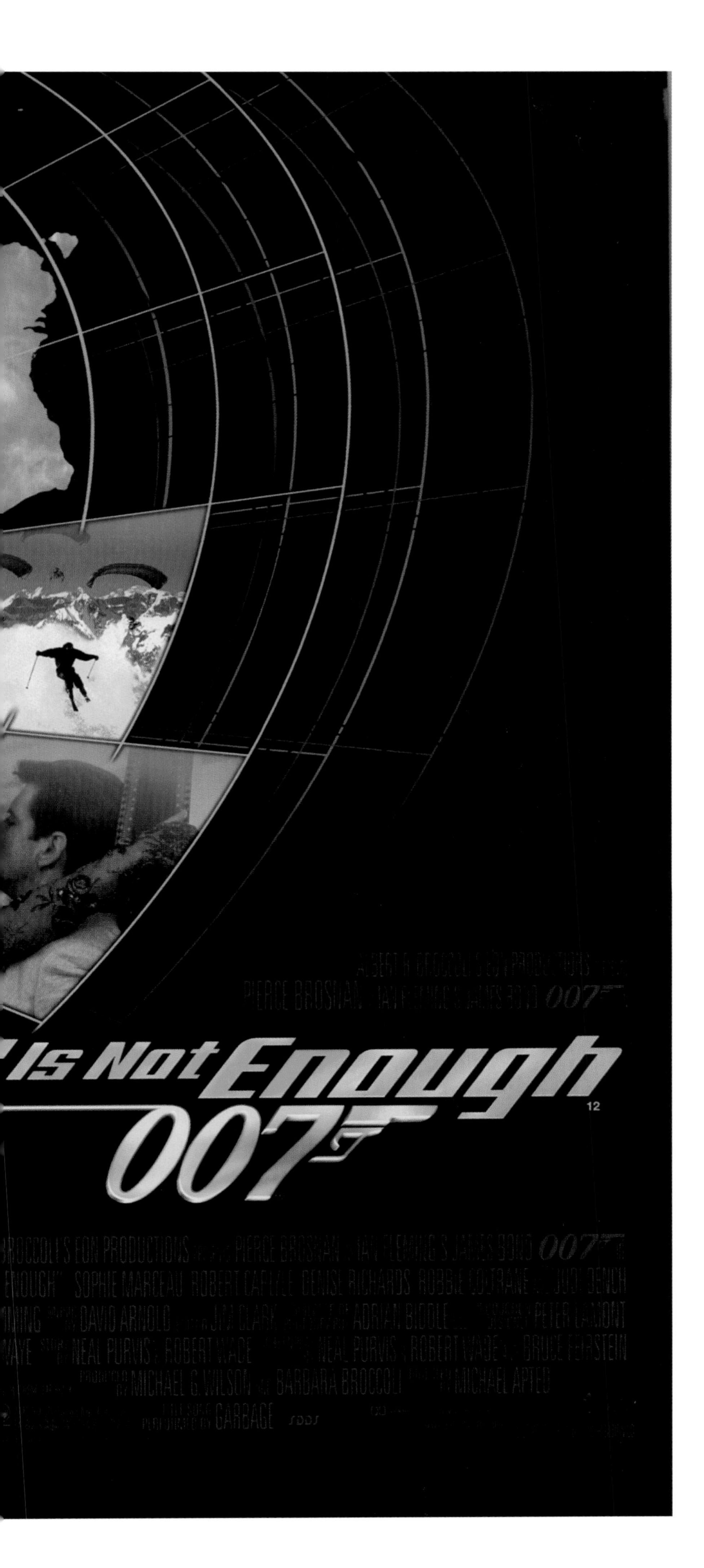

1999

The World Is Not Enough

Brosnan's third and highly successful Bond film, *The World Is Not Enough* returned to Pinewood Studios, and Bond production designer Peter Lamont came back to the fold, having been awarded an Oscar for his work on the blockbuster *Titanic*. Director Michael Apted focused on the emotional character of Bond in a more personal storyline.

After the murder of British oil magnate Sir Robert King by international terrorist Renard, his daughter Elektra inherits her father's empire of oil deposits. Prompted by Renard's burgeoning interest in her empire, Bond is sent to the Caucasus Mountains to protect Elektra from a possible attempt on her life. Despite his efforts, he discovers that Elektra has actually been working alongside Renard to plot the death of her father. Their evil plan is to detonate a nuclear submarine and thereby pollute the Bosphorus to such a degree that only her company would have the resources to minimize the resulting environmental disaster and so hold the world to ransom.

A US and international one-sheet were created for the campaign. The international one-sheet was then further refined by certain territories, in order to cater to the idiosyncrasies of their marketplace. For example, in the French version of the poster, Sophie Marceau is more prominent in the composition. The campaign used photographic images manipulated by computer, as opposed to illustrations drafted by the likes of McGinnis and Peak. The advance poster, featuring a clever use of the silhouette of Bond and a 'flame girl', had obviously been inspired by Maurice Binder's seminal work. This image has become known as one of the best Bond posters from the entire series.

British 30 x 40 in (76 x 102 cm)
Art Director Brian Bysouth
Creative Director Robin Behling
Photographers Nigel Parry, Keith Hamshere & Jay Maidment
Date of release November 1999

British 41 x 27 in (104 x 69 cm)
(International advance)
Designer Diane Reynolds
Creative Director Randi Braun

British 41 x 27 in (104 x 69 cm)
Designer Diane Reynolds
Creative Director Randi Braun
Photographers Nigel Parry, Keith Hamshere & Jay Maidment
Date of release November 1999

US 41 x 27 in (104 x 69 cm)
(Advance)
Designer Diane Reynolds
Creative Director Randi Braun

007
11 19 99

British 12 x 8 in (31 x 21 cm)
(Concept art produced in UK for international territories' in-theatre display)
Photographer Keith Hamshere
Note: original conceptual artwork is of rough quality

British 11 x 7 in (28 x 19 cm)
(Concept art produced in UK for international territories' in-theatre display)
Photographer Nigel Parry
Note: original conceptual artwork is of rough quality

British 15 x 9 in (36 x 24 cm)
(Concept art produced in UK for international territories' in-theatre display)
Photographer Nigel Parry
Note: original conceptual artwork is of rough quality

British 14 x 9 in (36 x 24 cm)
(Concept art produced in the US by Randi Braun)
Photographer Nigel Parry
Note: original conceptual artwork is of rough quality

Pierce Brosnan as
james bond
007
The World Is Not Enough

British 15 x 9 in (36 x 24 cm)
(Concept art produced in the US by Randi Braun)
Photographer Nigel Parry
Note: original conceptual artwork is of rough quality

British 15 x 9 in (36 x 24 cm)
Photographer Nigel Parry
Note: original conceptual artwork is of rough quality

Sophie Marceau as
elektra king
007
The World Is Not Enough

British 11 x 7 in (28 x 19 cm)
(Concept art produced in UK for Danish territories' in-theatre display)
Photographer Keith Hamshere
Note: original conceptual artwork is of rough quality

British 11 x 7 in (28 x 19 cm)
(Concept art produced in UK for German territories' in-theatre display)
Photographer Keith Hamshere
Note: original conceptual artwork is of rough quality

British 11 x 7 in (28 x 19 cm)
(Concept art produced in UK for Italian territories' in-theatre display)
Photographer Keith Hamshere
Note: original conceptual artwork is of rough quality

MARIA GRAZIA CUCINOTTA as
CIGAR GIRL
007
The World Is Not Enough
UNITED INTERNATIONAL PICTURES

British 14 x 9 in (36 x 25 cm)
(Concept art produced in the US by Randi Braun)
Photographer Keith Hamshere
Note: original conceptual artwork is of rough quality

British 14 x 9 in (36 x 25 cm)
(Concept art produced in the US by Randi Braun)
Photographer Nigel Parry
Note: original conceptual artwork is of rough quality

Robert Carlyle as
renard
007
The World Is Not Enough

French 63 x 47 in (160 x 120 cm)
(Final artwork)

Italian 55 x 39 in (140 x 99 cm)
Designer Gavino Sanna
Date of release January 2000

UNITED INTERNATIONAL PICTURES
GAVINO SANNA ASSOCIATI
Devi avere proprio
un buon motivo
per non vedere il nuovo
film di James Bond.
Il Mondo Non Basta
007
Dal 14 Gennaio nei migliori cinema.

Esquire posters

Before the release of *Thunderball* and *You Only Live Twice*, *Esquire* magazine did features on these titles. These articles introduced readers to the upcoming Bond girls, gadgets, villains and lavish sets. United Artists were able to use these features as the basis for creating these unusual advance posters.

US 60 x 40 in (152 x 102 cm)
(Esquire advance)

US 60 x 40 in (152 x 102 cm)
(Esquire advance)

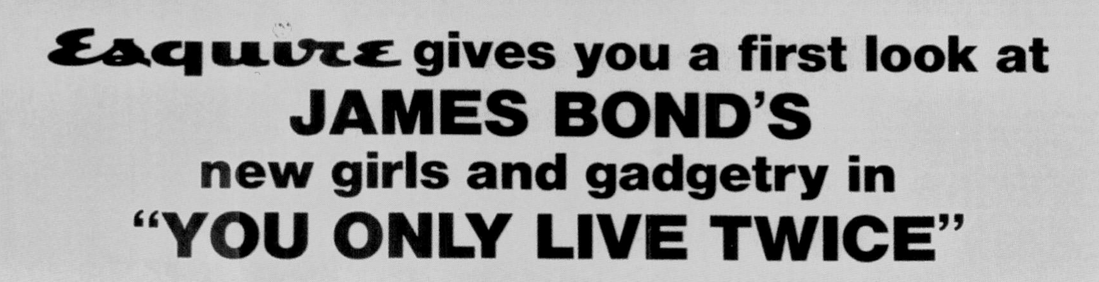

YOUR ATTENTION, PLEASE!

Twenty months ago, you thrilled to the profound mixture of sex, violence and gadgetry we presented in a preview of the James Bond movie, Thunderball. Since then you have slipped into the doldrums and longed for more vicarious thrills.

Well, guess what? There is a new Bond movie acoming. You Only Live Twice, and we have it for you. The big difference, though, is that this one starts out with James Bond getting killed!

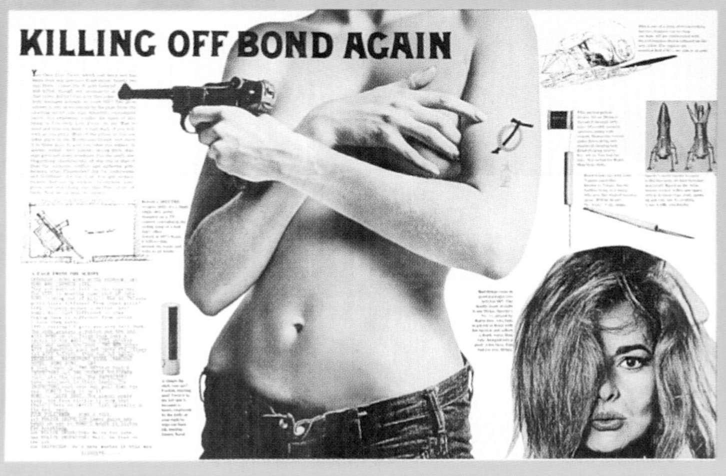

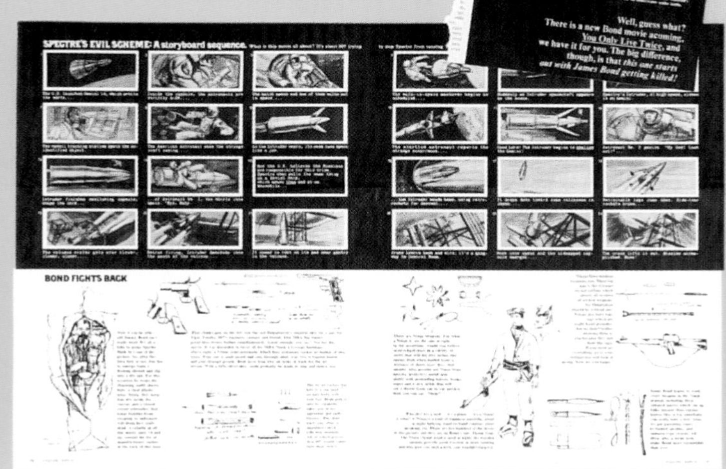

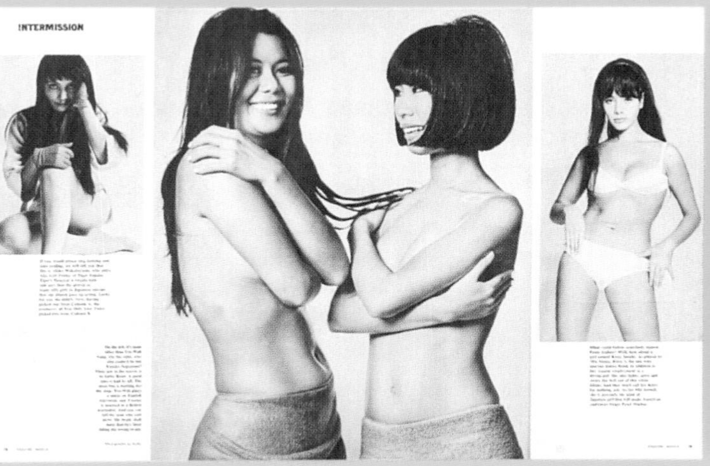

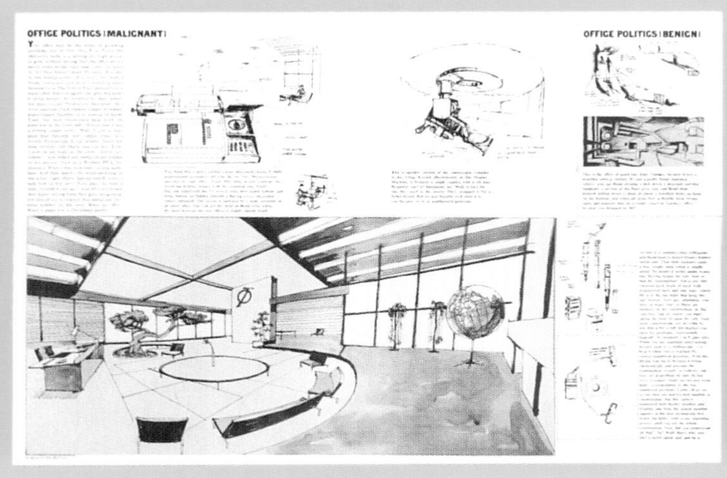

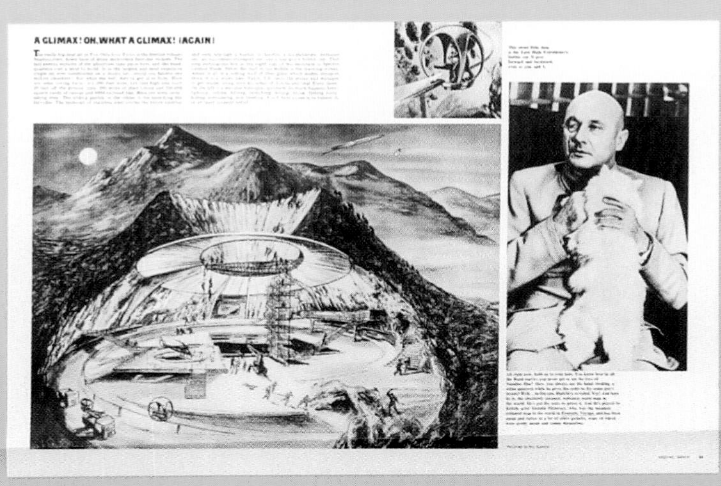

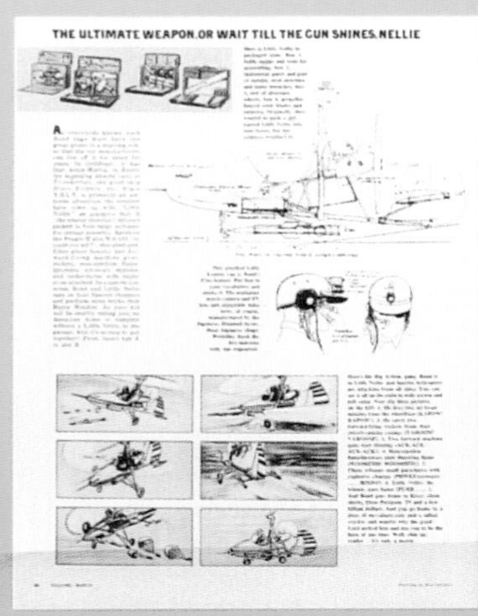

SEAN CONNERY IS JAMES BOND

IN IAN FLEMING'S "YOU ONLY LIVE TWICE"

Presented by ALBERT R. BROCCOLI and HARRY SALTZMAN · Directed by LEWIS GILBERT · Screenplay by ROALD DAHL · Produced by ALBERT R. BROCCOLI and HARRY SALTZMAN

Music by JOHN BARRY · Production designed by KEN ADAM

PANAVISION® · TECHNICOLOR® · Released thru UNITED ARTISTS

Festival posters

From as early as *Goldfinger*, cinemas worldwide had James Bond seasons. These shows played to packed audiences who would return to see the films over and over again. Special promotional posters were printed in limited quantities for each festival.

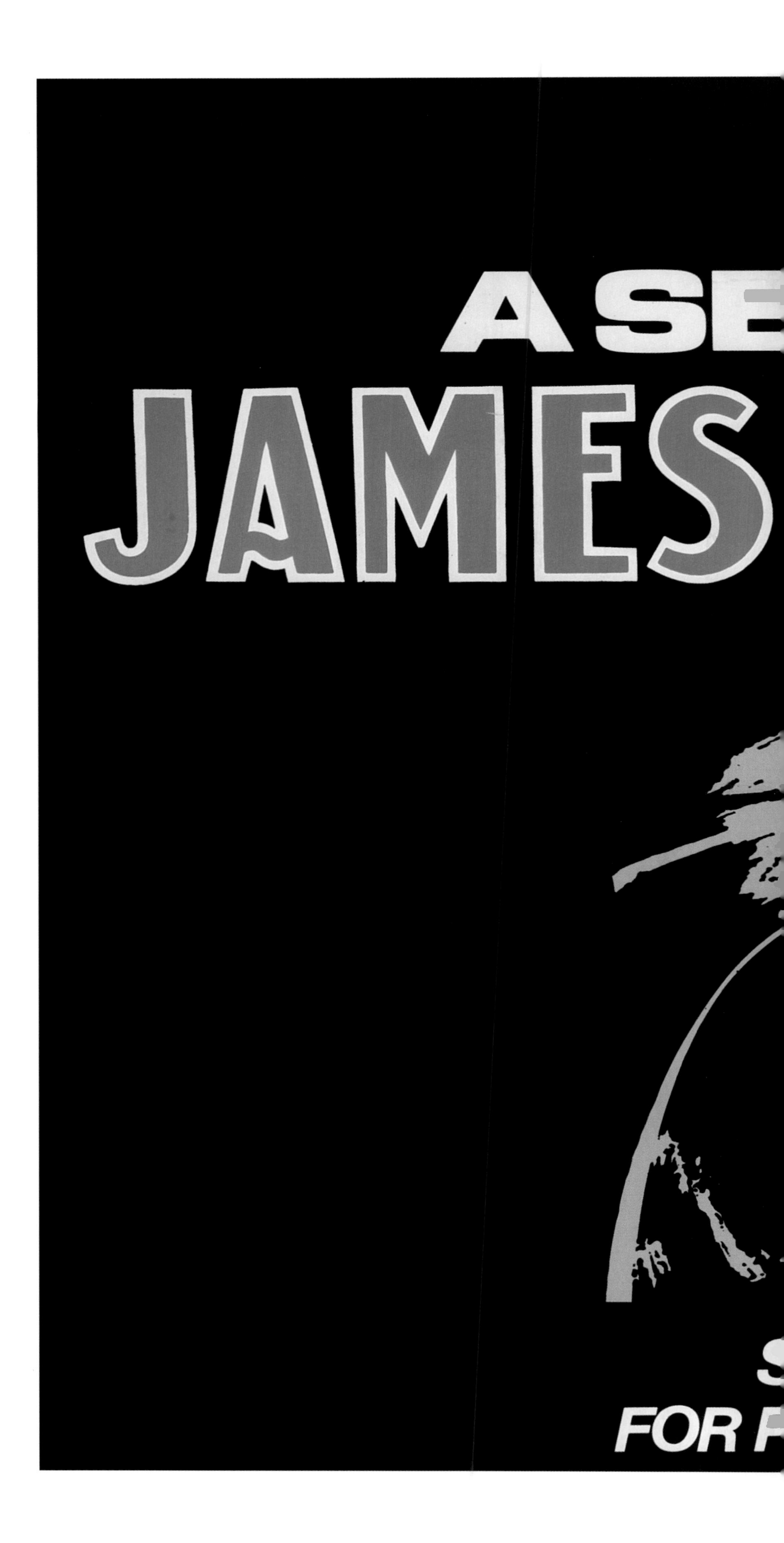

British 30 x 40 in (76 x 102 cm)
(Festival poster)
c1980s

ASON OF

BOND 007

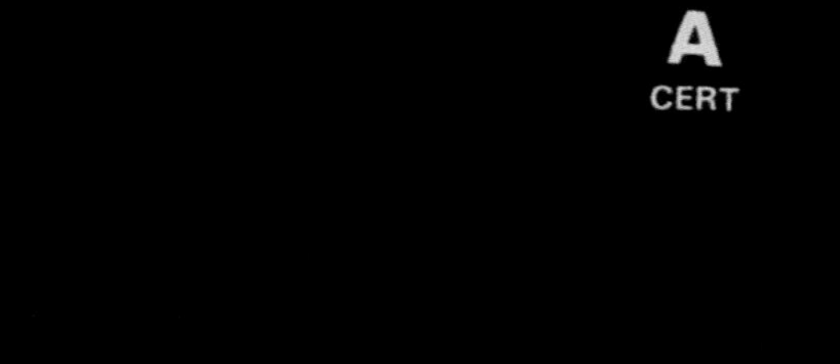

A
CERT

E LOCAL PRESS
OGRAMME DETAILS

US 28 x 22 in (56 x 71 cm)
(Unused festival poster)
1982

US 41 x 27 in (104 x 69 cm)
(Festival poster)
Featuring design by David Chasman
1972

Italian 79 x 55 in (201 x 140 cm)
(Festival poster)
Artist/Illustrator Averardo Ciriello
1972
Translation: *Everybody Against James Bond*

TUTTI CONTRO JAMES BOND

AGENTE 007
LICENZA DI UCCIDERE

AGENTE 007
DALLA RUSSIA CON AMORE

AGENTE 007
MISSIONE GOLDFINGER

AGENTE 007
THUNDERBALL (OPERAZIONE TUONO)

AGENTE 007
SI VIVE SOLO DUE VOLTE

AGENTE 007
AL SERVIZIO SEGRETO DI SUA MAESTA'

Artist Profiles

Gosta Aberg
From the 1930s to the 1970s, Aberg was one of the most prolific poster artists in Sweden, his work characterized by the use of unusual combinations of artwork and film stills. His other works include the Swedish posters for *The Wolf Man* (1941), *The Seventh Seal* (1957) and *Breakfast at Tiffany's* (1961). He was responsible for the Swedish designs of *Dr. No* and *Goldfinger*.

Randi Braun
Randi Braun is Senior Vice President – Creative Advertising for MGM/United Artists and has been responsible for overseeing the creation and implementation of print advertising campaigns for *GoldenEye*, *Tomorrow Never Dies* and *The World Is Not Enough*. An award-winning designer, she has developed print campaigns for every major film studio and most of the smaller US independent distributors. Her credits include campaigns for *Batman*, *The Godfather Part III* and *Indecent Proposal*.

Robert Brownjohn
Brownjohn was an influential graphic designer responsible for the main title sequences of *From Russia With Love* and *Goldfinger*. He also designed the British poster campaign for *Goldfinger* using two images of the Golden Girl, onto which were projected the figures of James Bond and Pussy Galore. A full-length body shot of the Golden Girl was also used in campaigns around the world, usually with a strategically placed image of Bond to avoid any embarrassment, and to protect her modesty. The second design of the British Quad for *Goldfinger* features a gold hand in place of the torso.

Renato Casaro
Italian poster artist Casaro was born in Treviso in 1935 before moving to Rome to work for the Studio Favalli, where, he worked with many other talented film poster artists. His creations for the Bond poster campaigns consist of the German poster for *Never Say Never Again* and the main campaign for *Octopussy*. Casaro is one of the most commercially successful illustrators working today. His poster for *The Last Emperor* was awarded a Key Art Award by the Hollywood Reporter. Since the 1960s, he has worked and lived in Germany.

David Chasman
Chasman was the Creative Director of United Artists and was responsible for the first Bond poster campaign, *Dr. No*. He hired the talent of Mitchell Hooks who created the much-celebrated image of Sean Connery with a cigarette in one hand and a smoking pistol in the other. Chasman also hired Joseph Caroff who created the famous 007 logo.

Averardo Ciriello
Ciriello was born in Milan in 1918. He began to paint film posters after the Second World War, working on titles such as *Spellbound* (1945), *The Outlaw* (1950), and later *The Apartment* (1960) as well as James Bond films. He is responsible for a fine painting used on the Italian posters for *From Russia With Love*, which depicts Connery and Daniela Bianchi in a slightly different pose to the usual design. For *Thunderball* Ciriello created a variation on an unused McGinnis concept. Ciriello's initial design featured Sean Connery without any shorts. Despite being a controversial image, the artwork was used, with the addition of a modicum of clothing.

Atelier Degen
A German design group, which was responsible for the German campaign for *Dr. No*. They used a painting of Sean Connery on two posters for the original campaign, and later used a second version for the 1965 re-release. All three posters were photomontages, combining photography and original artwork.

Vic Fair
Fair is known for his concept design and illustration, in particular for his advertising designs for *The Man Who Fell To Earth* (1976). He was the first designer to put Bond in a white tuxedo, a move that was accepted with restrained enthusiasm, leading to a small print run, and an alternative design being mainly used for the British campaign of *A View To A Kill*. However, the design worked to the extent that it created a strong visual impact due to the contrast of Moore in the white tuxedo and Grace Jones, standing behind him.

Renato Fratini
Fratini was responsible for the British campaign for *From Russia With Love*. The design, conceived by Eric Pulford and painted by Renato Fratini, originally featured an image of Sean Connery with a cruel expression. This was later changed in favour of a wry smile. Fratini's rendering of Connery with his pistol held diagonally across his chest has become one of the most instantly recognizable Bond images.

Bill Gold
Bill Gold has designed and conceived almost 2,000 film posters in the last fifty years. The first design campaign in which he participated was for the timeless *Casablanca* (1942). Back then, film advertising was held in poor regard, as Gold recalls: 'In the days when I started in the business, not many people wanted to do movie posters because they were considered trashy.' Bill Gold's long-standing collaboration with Clint Eastwood began in 1971, when he designed the posters for *Dirty Harry*. He has since been the poster designer for all Eastwood films. In fact, the poster Bill Gold designed for the Academy Award-winning *Unforgiven* (1992) was singled out of 5,000 entries by the Hollywood Reporter as the best American language poster of 1992. Striving to create clean, bold images that instantly tell a story, Gold's creations are guided by the modernist aesthetic that less is more. Gold's contribution to the Bond story came in the shape of the main campaign for *For Your Eyes Only*, an audacious design featuring scenes from the film and a striking visual arrangement of long legs and a crossbow.

Macario Gomez (Mac)
A Spanish poster designer who designed posters for titles such as the British poster for *Gunfight At The OK Corral* (1957), Gomez was also responsible for the Spanish campaigns of *Dr. No* and *From Russia With Love*. Gomez's design for the original release poster for *Dr. No* consisted of artwork of three girls with Bond in a violent action pose at the centre. Later, the 1974 re-release of the film re-used the surrounding portraits of the girls around a central image of Bond, this time in what had become known as the typical 007 pose - Bond and his gun - popularized by the poster for *From Russia With Love*. Gomez was also responsible for the Spanish campaign for *From Russia With Love*, which consisted of an oil painting designed as a series of vignettes from the film arranged around a central portrait of Bond.

Dan Gouzee
This New York-based artist was responsible for the artwork of two Bond poster campaigns, *Moonraker* (1979) and *A View To A Kill* (1985). Gouzee collaborated with Donald Smolen and on poster campaigns for films such as *Enemy Mine* (1985) and *The Mission* (1986). In 1979, Gouzee supplied the artwork for the James Bond challenge to the recent success of *Star Wars* (1977). The Teaser poster for *Moonraker* evoked the film's space theme wonderfully, with an image that worked to best effect on the British Quad for the film, due to its horizontal format. His campaign for *A View To A Kill* consisted of two images. The first was a painting of Grace Jones and Roger Moore, the other an action-style representation of Tanya Robert and Christopher Walken. Gouzee's images were used in a series of campaigns around the world.

Boris Grinsson
Grinsson was born in Germany in 1907, and fled to France when Hitler came to power. His career spans many decades, from the 1930s to the 1970s, and his delicate painterly style set him apart from many of his contemporaries. His most famous artworks include the French posters for *The Wizard Of Oz* (1939), *The Lady From Shanghai* (1948), *400 Blows* (1959) and *The Birds* (1963). His style was one perfectly suited to convey the elegance of Connery's James Bond, and it worked to great effect in the French posters for *Dr. No* and *From Russia With Love.*

Jean Mascii
Mascii is a French poster designer who was born in 1926. He created many French poster campaigns for American Westerns in the 1950s before finding fame designing posters for films such as *Plein Soleil* (1959) and *Alphaville* (1965). Mascii's finely detailed artwork reflects the aura of traditional French artwork, although his style also has a distinctly modern look. His work on the French posters for *Goldfinger* demonstrates a skilled painterly style.

Frank McCarthy
Frank McCarthy was born in New York City and educated first at the New York Art Student's League, and later at the Pratt Institute, where he majored in illustration. He started out as an illustrator for magazines such as *Colliers*, *Argosy* and *True*, as well as various paperback book publishers. McCarthy's first solo show in 1973 was a great success and sold out within twenty minutes of opening. In the mid-1970s, McCarthy moved to Arizona and began painting numerous works depicting scenes from the Wild West with an emphasis on action, and in doing so developed a much-acclaimed style. His film poster campaigns include *The Dirty Dozen* (1967), *Where Eagles Dare* (1968) and those for the Bond films, *Thunderball*, *You Only Live Twice* and *On Her Majesty's Secret Service*. In 1997, McCarthy was inducted into the Society of Illustrators Hall of Fame.

Robert McGinnis
In a career spanning over forty years, Robert McGinnis has distinguished himself as a painter of beautiful women and Western scenery. As a young man, the Cincinnati-born artist studied fine art at Ohio State University by day and commercial art at the Central Academy of Commercial Art by night. He began his career as an animation apprentice at Disney Studios, before moving on to film and advertising posters. He is responsible for no less than five Bond campaigns, as well over forty film posters, including *Breakfast At Tiffany's* (1961), *Barbarella* (1968) and *The Odd Couple* (1968). In his Bond campaigns, which included *Thunderball*, *On Her Majesty's Secret Service* and *Diamonds Are Forever*, McGinnis's style captured the essence of Bond glamour. After many years of creating book covers, film posters and portraits, McGinnis was inducted into the Society of Illustrators Hall of Fame, a Society that had awarded him accolades throughout his career. McGinnis's lifelong fascination with the Wild West led him to abandon movie poster art in the late 1970s, and to paint Western scenes, an expression of his childhood memories of growing up in rural Wyoming.

Bob Peak
The man known as the father of the modern movie poster was born in Denver, Colorado in 1927. Bob Peak studied at Wichita State University and later at The Art Center College of Design in Los Angeles. Peak was one of the USA's most prolific and respected illustrators and painters, his work ranging from postage stamps to fine art. He was responsible for over one hundred film poster designs, forty-five covers for *Time* magazine, and the British and US posters for *The Spy Who Loved Me*. His work informed the evolution of the approach to movie poster design from collage and photomontage of the stars to striking artistic illustrations. Peak's style is characterized by a use of shadow and light, and candy-coloured expressionistic backgrounds. His stylized portraits for films such as *Our Man Flint* (1966) and *Modesty Blaise* (1966) integrated decorative elements with representations of the stars. Peak was inducted to the Society of Illustrators Hall of Fame in 1977. His work for Bond films came as a result of the producers requesting something new and previously unseen. The design Peak produced for *The Spy Who Loved Me* combined a subtle Art-Deco image of Bond and Anya surrounded by futuristic elements.

Eric Pulford
Pulford began his career in film poster design in 1944. He was commissioned to design campaigns for Columbia, Rank, United Artists and Disney. Most famously, he collaborated with Renato Fratini for the British campaign for *From Russia With Love*. His other designs of note include the posters for *The Wages Of Fear* (1953), *Johnny Guitar* (1954) and *The Ipcress File* (1965).

Yves Thos
In a career spanning over forty years Thos was known for his illustrations for the French magazine *Pilote*, and also for creating French advertising images for brands such as *Uncle Bens*, *Coca-Cola*, and *Oasis*. Thos was also responsible for the outsized French poster for *On Her Majesty's Secret Service.*